Table of Contents

In the beginning . . .

In the Fall of 2017, I had the opportunity to teach a continuing education class at a local university. My subject was, *Unusual Percentage Increases in Price and Volume – Predicting Specific Stock Market Gainers.* Following that class, some of the folks who took that course requested that I arrange for regularly scheduled group meetings to continue discussions related to the discovery of stocks that offered the potential for above-average stock market performance.

Our original meetings were relatively unstructured, and discussions were typically intuitive, lacking useful metrics or screens that could be used repeatably to discover tomorrow's winning stocks . . . today. By July 2018, most of us had read *The Second Machine* Age and our continuing efforts had enabled us to discover valuable sources of research related to the Digital Transformation. Therefore, with this increased level of knowledge and confidence we decided to launch a model portfolio, designed to test our ability to discover stocks with extraordinary growth potential. Obviously, mistakes were made over the ensuing weeks and months but, overall, the performance since launch has conformed to the name we gave this portfolio – *Extraordinary Growth Stocks.*

One might even consider that the performance of our portfolio was indeed extraordinary. The following represents performance from the launch date of the model portfolio, July 1, 2018 until December 31, 2021:

S&P 500   + 76.2%

Nasdaq Composite   + 109.9%

EGS Portfolio + 225.3%

Percentages don't always resonate with many investors, so let's convert those percentages into dollars. If the original $500,000 had been invested into each of the market indexes and the EGS portfolio, the following shows the dollar values for the same period:

S&P 500 $881,000

Nasdaq Composite $1,049,500

EGS Portfolio $1,629,516

You can visit my website to learn the most recent end-of-month performance data for the above.

https://uvmetrics.com/

When looking at the performance numbers in the above, keep in mind that almost all institutional investment managers – including mutual funds and hedge funds – strive to match or beat the S&P 500 – and many *fail* to do so. Also, keep in mind that the Nasdaq Composite is heavily weighted towards technology stocks.

And then came the 2021-22 correction

As all investors know, market values rarely advance upward and to the right interminably. A steady stream of good news had generated euphoric expectations (greed) and market values become irrationally inflated. Stock market professionals carefully monitor these trends. They know that when the flow of good news abates – or when elements of negative news begin to appear – those irrationally inflated market values represent an alluring opportunity to profit by selling stocks short.

Selling stocks short reverses the normal investment procedure of first buying a specific stock low and then selling high. In contrast, short sellers sell a specific stock that they don't own at higher prices (they borrow stocks that they sell short from their brokerage firm), hoping that they can later buy those shares at lower prices and the brokerage firm can return the stocks to the original owners.

In late 2021 and early 2022, several negative macro-economic events began to dominate the financial news. Fears of inflation, rising interest rates, the Russian invasion of Ukraine, and supply-chain disruptions all contributed to a 20.9% decline in the S&P500 index and a 30.6% decline in the Nasdaq Composite. The latter, of course, is where most of the stocks involved with enabling the *Digital Transformation* are listed.

I can't predict that our investments will return to the end-of-year values indicated above, but our group has opted to remain invested in most of those stocks. If you are interested in following the performance of our investments, you can do so at my website . . . *https://uvmetrics.com/.*

I want to emphasize that you don't have to be a college graduate with a degree in finance or economics – nor do you have to be an expert in the arcane domain of stock chart analysis – to learn and to profit from the three stock discovery triggers presented in this book.

In fact, I often share with my subscribers that the discovery triggers are sort of like an Easter Egg Hunt in that the discovery process is a lot of fun. Almost all participants in an Easter Egg Hund *do* find eggs. Likewise, almost all participants following my methods *will* discover stocks with extraordinary growth potential.

Most importantly, in most instances you will be discovering stocks *before* most other individual investors – and in some instances, before institutional investors.

Not only will you have fun in your quest for discovering tomorrow's winning stocks – *today* – the process will also be a wonderful learning experience for you.

Introduction

"Advances in AI, machine learning, robotics, and other technologies have increased the pace of change tenfold. By 2025, we estimate that 50 billion devices will be connected to the Industrial Internet of Things (IIoT), while 70 percent of manufacturers are expected to be using digital twins regularly (by 2022). Some 70 percent of new applications will use LC/NC (Low Code/No Code) technologies by 2025, up from less than 25 percent in 2020. The global metaverse revenue opportunity could approach $800 billion in 2024, up from about $500 billion in 2020. This proliferation of technological innovations means we can expect to experience more progress in the next decade than in the past 100 years combined, according to entrepreneur and futurist Peter Diamandis."
2022-10-21 - *Tech at the edge: Trends reshaping the future of IT and business*

For many individuals the benefits attributed to the *digital transformation* might seem enigmatic. Our smart phones and tablets are digital, and they certainly have been transformative. However, it's in the corporate world where digital transformation has had its greatest impact and where the most meaningful benefits have been realized. From an investor's perspective, corporations that implement digital transformation strategies tend to outperform competitors in terms of viability, revenue growth and profitability, important considerations for all investors. Interestingly, a significant number of corporate benefits do flow through to consumers as measured by better service, better products and – in some instances – lower prices.

Consider the following:

"Across industries, change is happening in shorter waves than ever before, and CEOs feel the pressure but recognize the opportunity for the entire organization. Our research shows that leading companies in enterprise technology were growing two times faster than most companies, and by doubling down on their tech investments recently, they are now growing five times faster."

Why is Digital Transformation Important? – *Accenture*

"Data is a key pillar for digital transformation because every interaction in the digital world generates data. This data lets corporations create baselines and benchmarks for their transformation journey and provides a good indicator of progress.

Historically, this data was consumed for traditional reporting and analytics for stakeholders. However, thanks to today's rapidly changing market, corporations expect data to be:

• Delivered in real time for quick decision making.

• Able to generate intelligence in the form of predictive and prescriptive models for optimized operating models.

This requires the careful orchestration of a comprehensive data strategy that will allow corporate data to be discovered, analyzed and used to generate actionable insights for desired outcomes. Powerful machine learning and AI can generate models to assist with this process."

Data Is Essential to Digital Transformation – *Forbes*

If we can accept the concept that "data is a key pillar for digital transformation", we can then enhance our conviction based on the following:

*"Back in **2010** then Google CEO Eric Schmidt said 'From the dawn of civilization to 2003, five exabytes of data were created. The same amount of data was created in the last two days.'*

*Well, in **2020**, 59 zetabytes of data were created, which is 59,000 exabytes.*

*If 'from the dawn of civilization to 2003 five exabytes of data were created', then in 2020 **five exabytes were created every 45 minutes."***
Ophir Gottlieb, CML Pro

*"Data is what is driving innovation and business decisions, accelerating the development of products and services that quickly are finding their way into the hands of enterprises and consumers alike. It's also the scaffolding on which architectures are designed to ensure that data can be **collected, stored, and analyzed** as quickly as possible, regardless of the amount that is being generated or where it's created. It's like what oil has been for more than a century, a generator of vast amounts of value across the entire economy.*

While oil is available in ever diminishing quantities, the data universe is huge. What is great about this is that it's growing exponentially."
2020-7-21 - <u>Squeezing Every Drop of Value Out of Data</u> – The Next Platform

That term – ***growing exponentially*** – requires some further definition. The following has been extracted from Professors Erik Brynjolfsson and Andrew McAfee's seminal book, ***The Second Machine Age***, pps 45-50. The importance of the date *(2006)* mentioned towards the end of this article will become obvious as you continue to read.

"Our brains are not well equipped to understand sustained exponential growth. We severely underestimate how big the numbers can get. Inventor and futurist Ray Kurzweil retells an old story to drive this point home. The game of chess originated in recent-day India during the sixth century CE, the time of the Gupta Empire. As the story goes, it was invented by a very clever man who traveled to Pataliputra, the capital city, and presented his brainchild to the emperor. The ruler was so impressed by the difficult, beautiful game that he invited the inventor to name his reward.

The inventor praised the emperor's generosity and said, "All I desire is some rice to feed my family." Since the emperor's largess was spurred by the invention of chess, the inventor suggested they use the chessboard to determine the amount of rice he would be given. "Place one single grain of rice on the first square of the board, two on the second, four on the third, and so on," the inventor proposed, "so that each square receives twice as many grains as the previous."

"Make it so," the emperor replied, impressed by the inventor's apparent modesty.

After 32-squares, the emperor had given the inventor about 4 billion grains or rice. That's a reasonable quantity – about one large field's worth – but the emperor did start to take notice.

It was as they headed into the second half of the chessboard that at least one of them got into trouble.

Moore's Law and the tribble exercise allow us to see what the emperor did not: sixty-three instances of doubling yields a fantastically big number, even when starting with a single unit. If his request were fully honored, the inventor would wind up with more than eighteen quintillion grains of rice. A pile of rice this big would dwarf Mount Everest; it's more rice than has been produced in the history of the world. Of course, the emperor could not honor such a request.

*Kurzweil's distinction between the first and second halves of the chessboard inspired a quick calculation. Among other things, the U.S. Bureau of Economic Analysis (BEA) tracks American companies' expenditures. The BEA first noted "information technology" as a distinct corporate investment category in 1958. We took that year as the starting point for when Moore's Law entered the business world and used 18-months as the doubling period. **After 32 of these doublings, the U.S. businesses entered the second half of the chessboard when it comes to the use of digital gear. That was in 2006.***

If one graphed the progress of Moore's Law, it would have the exponential growth - *"hockey stick"* - appearance of the following:

Growth of $0.01 Doubling Daily

There's another way to illustrate exponential growth, one that is simpler and requires some imagination.

Imagine that you have accumulated extraordinary wealth and have decided to gift some of that wealth to a charity. Before making that gift, you want to test the ability of the charity to make wise, carefully thought-out decisions.

Here's the test: You offer the charity a choice. Either accept a gift of $1 million today, or accept the gift of $0.01 today, the value of which will double every day for the next 30-days. For example, on day two the value would be $0.02, day three $0.04, day four $0.08 and continuing that doubling for 30-days.

Most people would quickly opt for the $1 million today (a bird in the hand worth two in the bush!).

By the 15th day – halfway there – the value of the initial penny had grown to a mere $163.84, so a decision to accept the $1 million would appear to be quite wise. However, as with the grain of rice on the chess board, after day 15 the gains entered exponential growth.

By the 20th day the value of the penny had grown to $5,242.88 and by the 25th day, with just five days remaining, the value of the penny had grown to $167,772.16, and the doubling continued – very exponentially!

At the end of the 30-days the value of the original $0.01 had grown to **$5,368,709.12,** and a chart depicting that growth would have the same "hockey stick" appearance as Moore's Law.

Some extraordinary growth companies familiar to most of us, all launched within range of that 2006 date.

The following companies developed disruptive products or services within range of that 2006 date. *(Ages of the founders, when their companies were launched, are in parentheses.)*

Apple was founded in 1976 by Steve Jobs (21), Steve Wozniak (25) and Ronald Wayne (42). Although, in terms of founding date, Apple appears to be an outlier in this list, the product that has generated perhaps the greatest impact on our everyday lives – the ubiquitous **iPhone** – was introduced at the Macworld Expo on January 9, **2007**. It put the world in our pockets!

Netflix was founded in **1997** by Reed Hastings (37).

Google was founded in **1998** by Larry Page (25) and Sergey Brin (25).

Tesla was founded in **2003** by Elon Musk (32).'

Facebook was founded in **2004** by Mark Zuckerberg (20).

Twitter was founded in **2006** by Jack Dorsey (~30), Noah Glass (?), Biz Stone (32) and Evan Williams (44).

Airbnb was founded in **2008** by Brian Chesky (27), Joe Gebbia (27) and Nathan Bleccharczyk (25).

Uber was founded in **2009** by Garret Camp (31) and Travis Kalanick (25).

WhatsApp was founded in **2009** by Brian Acton (36) and Jan Koum (33).

Snapchat was founded **2011** by Evan Spiegel (21), Bobby Murphy (23) and Reggie Brown (?).

Perhaps the most striking feature in the above list is the age of the founders. These were not 50- or 60-year-old moguls meeting in Davos, Switzerland or The Greenbrier Resort in West Virginia to map the future of the world economies.

Rather, they were young men filled with an entrepreneurial spirit to do something that had never been done before. Their primary attributes were their understanding of the marvels of digital technologies and their entrepreneurial determination to solve existing problems. There was one other overarching characteristic – they all had an energizing vision of the benefits their products or services could bring to corporations and individuals.

For example, how many folks were clamoring for a smart phone prior to Apple's introduction of the iPhone back in 2007? The following is a terrific illustration of how some of these entrepreneurs were able to "think outside the box" to create unique products or services that subsequently became world-class – and achieved that status without a huge investment in tangible assets.

"In March of 2015, strategist Tom Goodwin pointed out a pattern. Uber, the world's largest taxi company, owns no vehicles. Facebook, the world's most popular media owner, creates no content. And Airbnb, the world's largest accommodation provider, owns no real estate."
<u>Machine, Platform, Crowd</u>, McAfee & Brynjolfsson, P. 6

An illustration of the investment possibilities using the metrics and research sources outlined in this book.

The data contained in the following illustration is certifiable. The investor, Harry Brown, is fictitious. The unusual/price/volume "trigger" metric used by Harry represents *just one* of the suggested metrics revealed in this book that you will easily learn to apply in your efforts to discover stocks with extraordinary growth potential.

On Friday, November 6, 2015, Nvidia's (NVDA) stock closed at $30.44. That closing price was 14% higher than Thursday's closing price. That percentage gain was truly extraordinary since the day-to-day closing prices of most stocks – as well as most market averages – seldom change more than one or two percent from one trading day to the next. Friday's volume of trading for NVDA was 29,306,777 shares which was 192% higher than NVDA's normal trading volume.

That combination – substantially higher percentage increases in both price and volume – was a clear signal that some investors were aggressively buying the stock. Furthermore, because of the extraordinary percentage increase in volume, the aggressive investors were probably savvy institutional investors who had apparently discovered some market moving information relative to NVDA.

Alerted by the forgoing data, Harry decided to visit NVDA's web site – specifically the section dedicated to *Investors*. There he learned that after the market closed on November 5th NVDA announced their financial results for the third quarter of fiscal 2016.

The following comments were included in that earnings announcement.

"Our record revenue highlights Nvidia's position at the center of forces that are reshaping our industry" said Jen-Hsun Huang, co-founder and chief executive officer of Nvidia. "Virtual Reality, deep learning, cloud computing and autonomous driving are developing with incredible speed, and **we are playing an important role in all of them.** *"*

Using the above information, Harry bought NVDA when the market opened on Monday, November 9th, at a cost of $31.28 per share. Let's assume that he bought 500 shares of NVDA at that price, for a total cost (less commissions) of $15,640.

Harry would soon learn that making his NVDA buy decision was one of the easiest decisions he would have to make. Knowing if and when to sell would later become an important decision for Harry.

On October 2, 2018, NVDA traded at a high of $73.19, representing a gain of 132% above the original purchase price. The next 2-months would become an investment nightmare for Harry. By December 24, 2018, the market price for NVDA traded at a low of $31.11, which was $0.17 *below* his original cost.

What happened to precipitate such is disastrous decline in market value? Fortunately, NVDA is one of those companies that communicates effectively with investors and Harry had signed up on the company's web site to receive regular news updates. In NVDA's November 18th 2019Q3 Financial Results press release, CEO Jensen Huang made the following comment:

"Our near-term results reflect excess channel inventory post the crypto-currency boom, which will be corrected. ***Our market position and growth opportunities are stronger than ever.*** *"*

What had happened to NVDA was an excessive build-up of inventory for the "crypto-currency" market, resulting in significant unsold, non-revenue producing inventory. The market chose to focus on the first sentence in the above quote and to ignore the second sentence.

However, what really spooked investors was that NVDA's year-over-year quarterly revenue growth – after averaging 48.1% over the previous 2-years – declined to 20.7% for 2019Q3. That 48.1% average revenue growth was obviously abetted by the growth of crypto currencies. When the revenue growth of that market declined, it resulted in slower revenue growth for NVDA.

However, as all investors know, the market is an anticipatory mechanism and in NVDA's case, that anticipation was spot on. For the next four quarters NVDA's year-over-year quarterly revenue growth was negative. The crypto currency excessive inventory caused negative year-over-year negative revenue growth for the ensuing four quarters..

However, in NVDA's 2020Q4 financial report, NVDA reported a 40.8% gain in year-overs-year quarterly revenue, resuming its previous extraordinary growth. That extraordinary growth would continue for the next seven quarterly reports, thereby confirming Huang's comment that "growth opportunities are stronger than ever."

Perhaps equally as important for Harry, during the week of February 10, 2020, NVDA hit a recovery high of $73.74 which was just a bit over the October 2018 high. That recovery occurred in just a little over one year.

Let's make another assumption. Let's assume that Harry had faithfully followed NVDA's dominant market leadership in some of the world's leading growth markets and remained convinced that the inventory correction was merely a bump in the road. That *perspective* – generated from a continuing analysis of information coming from NVDA and credible analysts – enabled Harry to maintain his investment in NVDA.

On December 31, 2021 NVDA's closing price was $294.11. At that price the total value of Harry's original investment of **$15,640** had grown to **$588,220** for a gain of ~~840%~~.   3,661%

"The stock market is a device for transferring **money** *from the* **im***patient to the patient."*

   Warren Buffet

Here's the chart for Nvidia's Revenue Growth and related Stock Market Prices: (*Note: Dates in the following chart reflect NVDA's Fiscal Year and are different from Calendar Year dates.*

Nvidia (NVDA)						
	Quarterly Revenue Analysis				Stock Market Prices	
FY		Report Date	Actual	Y/Y Change	Actual	% Change
2018	Q1	30-Apr-17	1,937		$26.18	
	Q2	30-Jul-17	2,230		$41.24	57.5%
	Q3	29-Oct-17	2,636		$50.47	92.8%
	Q4	28-Jan-18	2,911		$60.69	131.8%
2019	Q1	10-May-18	3,207	65.6%	$61.75	135.9%
	Q2	16-Aug-18	3,123	40.0%	$63.24	141.6%
	Q3	15-Nov-18	3,181	20.7%	$40.83	56.0%
	Q4	14-Feb-19	2,205	-24.3%	$40.74	55.6%
2020	Q1	16-May-19	2,220	-30.8%	$39.63	51.4%
	Q2	15-Aug-19	2,579	-17.4%	$39.84	52.2%
	Q3	14-Nov-19	3,014	-5.2%	$52.42	100.2%
	Q4	13-Feb-20	3,105	40.8%	$71.82	174.3%
2021	Q1	21-May-20	3,080	38.7%	$88.25	237.1%
	Q2	19-Aug-20	3,866	49.9%	$119.75	357.4%
	Q3	18-Nov-20	4,726	56.8%	$132.13	404.7%
	Q4	24-Feb-21	5,003	61.1%	$141.23	439.5%
2022	Q1	26-May-21	5,661	83.8%	$157.00	499.7%
	Q2	18-Aug-21	6,507	68.3%	$195.00	644.8%
	Q3	17-Nov-21	7,103	50.3%	$323.67	1136.3%
	Q4	16-Feb-22	7,643	52.8%	$235.00	797.6%

Stock Market Prices are taken from the Open Price on the day following the release of the Quarterly Financial Report. The % Change is the change from each Actual entry to the first, or original Actual of $26.18.

Although the market price of all stocks is affected by overall market movements, one can observe in the above chart how the Y/Y Change in Quarterly Revenues has a strong influence on Stock Market Prices. A trend in Revenue Growth will almost always create a trend in Stock Market Prices.

You might suggest that creating this illustration is easily done using hindsight. I would counter that by offering the following information. In early 2022 I recently called up the 250 best 5-year performing stocks as listed by *barchart*. Although NVDA was included in that listing, there were 41 stocks that had performed better.

After you have read – and applied – the discovery and research ideas in this book, your subsequent investment decisions may not match what Harry Brown achieved with NVDA. Be assured, however, that some of your investments will likely ***exceed*** that performance.

I am confident that you will become a smarter – and therefore better – investor.

Chapter 1 - Market Moving Information – the Driving Force of Market Trends

In the November 2012 issue of <u>Fortune</u> several financial gurus were asked to reveal the best investment advice they had ever received. One of the gurus was John Bogle, founder of the Vanguard Group of mutual funds. Here's his response to that question:

"I was a runner for a little brokerage firm here in Philadelphia, delivering securities from one little brokerage firm to another. One of the other runners looked at me and he said, "Bogle, I'm gonna tell you everything you need to know about the investment business." And I said, "What's that, Ray?" And he said, "Nobody knows nuthin'." And it turns out, Ray was right. People say there are great performers out there, but it's a lot of randomness. None of us are smarter than the markets."

The late Bogle was a highly respected visionary during his long career in the investment industry, but he was demonstrably wrong in stating that none of us is smarter than the markets. Stocks move higher or lower because some investors have discovered market moving information that portends future higher market values.

Those investors – especially the early discoverers – are probably random, but it is their buying that begins the trends that move market values higher. When these early discoverers accurately assess the positive impact that market moving information will have on a specific stock, they are indeed smarter than the markets.

Early discoverers can be either individual or institutional investors. Although the institutional investors usually provide the *oomph* that propels market values higher, individual investors – through networks of friends or business contacts – are quite often the earliest discoverers of market moving information.

Although individual discoverers are smarter than the markets insofar as the discovery process is concerned, institutional early discoverers are more capable of assessing the impact that the market moving information will have on the market value of stocks. That ability is a critical difference between individual investors and institutional investment management firms.

The gradual dissemination of market moving information is precisely the driving force of stock market trends.

Experienced investors know that market moving information should have the important dimension of scarcity value – that is, an insight that has not been widely disseminated will almost always have a higher investment value than if it has already been broadly disseminated.

Said differently, *the early bird gets the worm* – or, in this case, the early investors quite often earn the largest profits since they buy early at low prices and benefit from subsequent market price increases generated by growing buying demand as more and more investors learn about the market moving information.

As mentioned, the challenge for early discoverer investors is to discover market moving information as close to the source of that information as possible. That's easier said than done. Becoming an early discoverer of market moving information will normally represent a difficult challenge for most individual investors, particularly those who pursue investing as an avocation and not as a dedicated full-time effort.

So, where does market moving information originate?

Obviously, market moving information originates with corporate insiders – the Board of Directors, officers and employees who are responsible for conceiving and developing the products or services that generate extraordinary growth.

However, Regulation Full Disclosure (Reg FD) – enacted by the SEC in August 2000 – mandates that when companies disclose material, nonpublic information, they must disseminate that information broadly to all investors, individuals as well as institutions. Therefore, those originators of market moving information – generally referred to as insiders – are no longer a legal source for that information.

Fortunately for investors who aspire to be early discoverers of market moving information, there are alternatives. Proof of the existence of those alternatives is that trending stocks are clearly apparent in all market environments. If Reg FD was truly efficacious, market moving information would be made available simultaneously to all investors. Hence, there would be no trends.

An Illustration – The Initial Steps of Upward Market Trends

There can be no possible justification for putting our money in stocks if we do not have some reasonable and rational belief that prices will generally go up over time.

Warren Buffet

Let's assume that you have a brother-in-law who works as a quality inspector for More Power Corp (MPC), a publicly owned company that has developed a revolutionary new microprocessor that exponentially increases the performance of the current state-of-the-art microprocessors. The product is in early production mode and orders for the product are streaming into MPC. Production lines are being expanded and MPC is aggressively hiring new employees.

If he doesn't have stock options your brother-in-law will probably buy some MPC stock for himself and his immediate family. He will probably share some of the company's good news with his relatives, including you. Obviously, you will also buy some MPC stock.

Repeat this process with other company employees and you can see that the discovery process begins with a trickle as family members and friends all decide to buy MPC stock. The information dissemination process will eventually become viral as each new investor shares his or her anticipated wealth-building experience with friends and relatives.

Initially all these buy orders are probably sent through a local stockbroker or investment advisor. If the information is credible and compelling, the investment advisor will join the cascading buy orders and buy MPC stock for himself or herself. He or she would then call many of his or her clients to suggest that they also buy some MPC stock.

All these orders would ultimately be sent from the investment advisor's firm to a brokerage firm that made a market in MPC stock – somewhat like a central marketplace that specialized in handling buy and sell orders for MPC stock.

Market makers do more than just accommodate buyers and sellers. The increased buying activity would alert the market maker to the fact that something special was happening at MPC. Most important, every one of those buy orders meant that the market maker had to find existing MPC shareholders who might be interested in selling their stock (for every buyer, there must be a seller).

As market prices gradually increase there will be a normal tendency among some of the early investors to sell their stock to "nail down" profits.

To unearth additional potential sellers the market maker might contact MPC directly – for two reasons. First, the market maker could request a list of current shareholders from MPC – they would represent potential sellers. The second reason for contacting MPC is less obvious. Like most new companies MPC probably attracted key employees by offering them stock options in lieu of high salaries. One way for the key employees to achieve higher income is to sell some of their stock options. Therefore, they become a good source of stock that might be available for sale to offset the growing buy orders.

Also, it's in MPC's best interest to cooperate with the market maker by providing him/her with general information that would not be considered insider information. For example, if the local newspaper or a trade magazine had issued a story about MPC the company would be sure that the market maker had access to those stories. MPC might also be willing to confirm that they are aggressively hiring new employees. In many ways, the market maker would ultimately have more generic information about MPC than any other source.

In addition, the market maker would likely see an investment opportunity in MPC, for the market maker's firm and for principals of the firm. Obviously, the firm would earn commissions or profit from the spread between bid and asked prices for MPC stock. To illustrate, they might buy shares from sellers at perhaps $4.00 and then resell those shares to buyers at $4.50 a share, thereby earning $50 on every 100-share order.

It's reasonable to assume that they would also buy MPC for their own investment portfolio. Buying MPC for their own investment portfolio does involve an element of risk for the market makers, and they try to mitigate that risk by learning more about the company before committing the firm's money. The market maker is typically in constant contact with buyers and buyers' brokers as well as with MPC. They can and will ask why folks are buying MPC. If nothing more, they can ask MPC to verify or deny the legitimacy of those reasons for buying MPC stock. They represent one of the first reasonably thorough research analyses of MPC, albeit they seldom are as sophisticated and thorough as institutional investment management firms.

Legitimate Sources for Market Moving Information in the Real World

Companies don't exist in a vacuum. A lot of what corporations do during the normal course of operations is visible or can be easily learned. For example, all companies have suppliers, customers, and/or competitors. Key suppliers that provide a company with raw materials or important services will certainly be aware of increased sales to a company experiencing extraordinary growth. Customers or retailers who buy the emerging company's products or services for resale to others – whether retailers or wholesalers – will obviously be aware of accelerating demand for those products or services. And alert competitors will sooner or later be aware of the revenues being diverted or lost from their own products or services to the new competition.

Other sources of market moving information might include independent industry consultants and writers for magazines and newspapers that focus on specific industries. In addition, every major corporation has a competitive intelligence department that analyzes trends within their industry and significant product development or new marketing strategies occurring at competitive companies. Any company that is *not* aware of new product or service developments by companies within its industry risks the very real possibility of obsolescence.

Finally, the search by institutional investment management firms and hedge funds for market moving information that does not violate Reg FD has become so compelling that a relatively new industry has been created – the *Expert Network* industry. The companies within this new industry are essentially match-makers, introducing industry experts to institutional investment professionals. The fees charged for these introductions are beyond reasonable for most individual investors.

Virtually every one of these alternative sources does not violate Reg FD. Furthermore, other than corporate insiders, very few people are more aware of industry trends or consequential advances being made by companies within that industry.

None of these early discoverers will ring any bells to announce their discovery of market moving information. Rather, the dissemination will often follow a path of conversation with friends, cocktail party conversation, internet blogs, local and regional media reports, cable news, network news, and finally daily, weekly and monthly publications.

This dissemination begins as a trickle, but the process soon becomes viral as an increasing number of potential investors share the information. Most important, at some point along this path the folks on Wall Street learn about market moving information and at that point significant volume increases typically occur.

The consequence of the dissemination process is often manifested in an increase in daily trading volume and an upward stock market trend. As will be seen in subsequent chapters, those manifestations can quickly and easily be detected by astute investors, whether they be institutional or individual. Most important, the lion's share of the profits generated by market trends goes to those investors who buy during the early stages of those trends.

The Next Step That Corroborates Genuine Upward Trends

Two essential features that characterize sustainable upward trends are missing during the early days of discovery by friends, relatives and local brokerage firms. Those two features are provided only by institutional investment management firms and hedge funds. They are:

Quantity and quality of research.

The quantity, the quality and the credibility of investment research provided by the major Wall Street brokerage firms to discover and profit from the discovery to tomorrow's winning stocks – *today* - is widely recognized as being incomparable. Consider the following:

"Goldman Sachs is one of the world's biggest investment banks, but it is arguably also a major technology company. About a third of the firm's employees are engineers. With hundreds of thousands of cloud computing processors working on its behalf, Goldman crunches more data each day than many Internet companies.

Our core business isn't software from a classical perspective, but we are massively digitized. We run almost an [Amazon Web Services] within Goldman Sachs because we have thousands of mission-

critical applications that have helped us drive change in the financial services business."
Meet the Internet's Newest Cloud Startup: Goldman Sachs? <u>The Information</u>, *October 15, 2014*

All the nation's largest institutional investment management firms have the experience and analytic capabilities like those of Goldman Sachs.

Not only can they identify sectors of the economy that are likely to grow fastest, but they can also identify companies within those sectors that are likely to be the most profitable. Most important, an analyst covering a specific industry is likely to be in contact with most of the leading companies within that industry, so their awareness and knowledge of market moving information within that industry are certifiably better than most other investors.

Individual investors rarely have the experience and the analytic capabilities to perform the quantity and quality of research performed by the larger institutional investment management firms. Perhaps the most insurmountable challenge for individual investors is the inability to forecast potential future earnings – both in terms of what those earning might be and when they might occur.

Quarterly Revenues and Earnings

These are key metrics, since, without them, it's difficult – if not impossible – to project future or even current fair market values.

This step is critical and it explains why stocks often move steadily higher once institutional investors begin their buying programs. Most individual investors simply don't have the knowledge and the experience to assess the impact that new companies, new products, or new services will have within an existing industry. And, even if they could assess that impact, converting that knowledge into an assessment of future revenues and earnings for a specific company would rarely have the same credibility – and therefore market impact – as a similar assessment done by an institutional investment management firm or a hedge fund.

Furthermore, only these large institutional investors can afford to access the prohibitively expensive *expert networks* that provide industry insights, such as new products or new marketing strategies that have recently occurred within specific industries.

Finally, those research efforts and analyses are on-going during the entire time of institutional ownership. Collectively these firms spend billions of dollars each year seeking market moving investment information

Buying volume.

Institutional investors know that they must make significant "bets" to generate above-average investment returns. And, make no mistake about this, the competition among institutional investment management firms is intense, with the critical competitive differential being performance. Instead of buying hundreds of shares that typify individual purchases, institutions typically execute their orders using block trades, acquiring thousands of shares – or more – in each transaction.

Buying ten thousand or twenty thousand shares of a company's stock is insignificant to most institutional investors. They must acquire hundreds of thousands of shares, often millions of shares, to have an impact on their overall performance.

To accumulate the total number of shares that they ultimately want to own, institutional investors spread their purchases over time. Consider, for example, the market consequences if an institution wanted to own five million shares of a company whose daily trading volume averaged just 100,000 shares a day. Trying to buy the entire five million shares in one trading day would likely cause a sharp increase in that company's stock market price. To avoid that sort of market value spike – and paying an unnecessarily higher price - institutions will typically spread their purchases over time.

As you will learn later in this book, savvy individual investors can take advantage of institutional investors spreading their purchase programs over a limited period. When one considers that more than one institutional investor is likely to be pursuing the same buying procedure, the advantage to individual investors is thereby magnified.

An illustration of why those two features are important.

Let's go back to MPC and the purchases made by those original investors. Let's assume that the average per share cost for all those individuals was around $5.00 per share. Over the next weeks and months, the price might have increased to perhaps $10.00 a share and each of those investors probably would have been ecstatic about those gains.

Contrast that level of ecstasy with the following prognosis developed by institutional investors and you can readily see that ultimately the early ecstasy perhaps turned to utter frustration if they happily sold their stock with a gain of 100% or slightly more.

Once institutional investment management firms and hedge funds have cranked up their research on MPC, future revenues and earnings can usually be credibly computed. Armed with the results of those computations, those professional investors can project future stock market valuations by ascribing a future credible price-to-earnings ratio.

To illustrate, if the projections suggest that in 3-years MPC's earnings per share would be $3.50 to $4.00 per share, and that earnings growth could be reasonably projected even beyond that 2-year period, a 20-price-to-earnings ratio would probably seem reasonable. Therefore, these professional investors can comfortably project a market value of $70 to $80 per share within 3-years.

If the stock was currently trading at $10 per share one can readily see the potential for the development of a very strong bullish trend. Consider this: If a fund manager at Fidelity managed a fund with assets in excess of $10 billion and he identified a stock with the price appreciation potential mentioned in the preceding paragraph, do you think he or she would be content buying 1,000 or even 10,000 shares?

When one recognizes that Fidelity would not be the only institutional investment manager to identify and research the revenue and earnings potential for MPC, one can readily understand the significant market appreciation potential.

What we have just described is the beginning and evolution of a strong bullish trend. Discovering that trend early – perhaps as in the above illustration when Fidelity launched their buying campaign of MPC – is both realistically possible and hugely rewarding for individual investors.

The institutional investor *dis*advantage

As mentioned above, one of the more interesting aspects of institutional buying is that quite often they can't acquire all the stock they eventually want to own in just one transaction. These parceled-out institutional investment trades provide an important advantage to individual investors. To wit, they typically generate clear signals of ***unusual daily percentage increases in price and volume***. When several institutional investment management firms or hedge funds decide to pursue the same stock within roughly the same time frame, those unusual price and volume signals become unmistakable. When that occurs, individual investors should prepare themselves for a delightful, wealth-building ride.

The challenges for individuals making investment decisions

Everybody's been talking about the late Steve Jobs. You see, Steve Jobs wasn't meeting needs; his company never met a need. Steve Jobs and his company created a need. Nobody knew they needed an iPhone. The same thing was true with the transistor and flight and Henry Ford's mass production of cars.

Businesses like the one Steve Jobs created and businesses like Intel and Microsoft and Amazon and Groupon and Facebook and eBay -- nobody else sees that stuff coming. Nobody else says, "Hey, we need a site where we can post pictures from the weekend. We need a site that's basically a 24/7 garage sale." That wouldn't have market

tested well. But look at Facebook and eBay -- they're multibillion-dollar companies that created jobs for thousands of people.
Q&A with Jim Clifton, CEO of Gallup and author of The Coming Jobs War

The above comment represents a conundrum for individual investors. Beginning in the mid-1980s a profusion of technology stocks experienced dramatic growth, developing and marketing products and services that were eagerly acquired by consumers and businesses.

However, if the underlying growth of revenues from companies like Apple could not be anticipated, how could individual investors decide to buy Apple stock – or the stock of any rapidly growing companies?

Lacking the comfort of knowing the extent of future growth potential it would surely seem reasonable that many investors would always think that it was too late to make an investment, that the growth train had already left the station.

Even when sequential quarterly earnings reports reveal a strong growth pattern in revenues, quarter-over-quarter and year-over-year, investors inevitably might question whether the future growth potential has already been factored into the price of the stock. And, lacking expert opinions and analyses, they question whether that growth is, in fact, sustainable going forward.

Under those circumstances, developing the confidence to "pull the trigger" and make an investment becomes a daunting challenge for most investors. Wondering whether the train of investment opportunity has already left the station causes some investors to defer deciding to invest.

In addition, in most instances the stock market value of companies that have developed new products or services can't be justified by normal investment analyses like price-to-earnings ratios since, for most emerging growth companies, there are no current earnings.

Further complicating the investment decision process, new technologies come in different flavors – solar energy, networking, social networking, e-commerce, biotechnology, satellite communications, search engines, etc. Very few individual investors have the broad technological knowledge to effectively analyze these various technologies or to assess the impact those technologies will have on other industries.

Therefore, deciding to invest in companies that are either contributing to or enabling the Digital Transformation becomes a leap of faith for most individual investors. Because their investments have been made based upon this leap of faith – rather than incisive and comprehensive analysis of future potential – they will lack the *perspective* that immunizes investors from the destructive emotions of fear and greed, the nemeses of successful investing.

As illustrated earlier, if future growth projections are credible, higher market values will almost certainly occur, but those higher values are miniscule compared to the trends that occur when savvy institutional investors jump in with their buying programs – programs that are predicated upon realistic projections of future revenues and earnings.

In the following chapters you will learn how to discover stocks that are either contributing to or benefiting from, the Digital Transformation. Said differently, you will learn how to effectively compete with – and often become more successful than - institutional investors in the quest for the discovery of tomorrow's winning stocks – ***today.***

.

Chapter 2 – The New Investment Era of Digital Transformation

"In terms of the internet, nothing has happened yet! The internet is still at the beginning of its beginning. It is only becoming. If we could climb into a time machine, journey 30 years into the future, and from that vantage look back to today, we'd realize that most of the greatest products running the lives of citizens in 2050 were not invented until after 2016."
The Inevitable, Kevin Kelly

. . "the confluence of four major technological forces – cloud computing, big data, artificial intelligence, and the internet of things – is causing a mass extinction event in industry after industry, leaving in its wake a growing number of organizations that have either ceased to exist or have become irrelevant."
Condoleezza Rice *–Foreword, Digital Transformation by Thomas M. Siebel*

The ascendance of technology in the investment world.

A common metric used to assess the success of a business venture is capitalization. That may sound like one of those enigmatic terms understood only by Wall Street regulars. In fact, it is quite simple to understand.

Capitalization measures the true worth of a company. It is calculated by multiplying the number of shares of a company's common stock issued and outstanding times the current stock market price. In simple terms, what it measures is the amount of money that would be required to buy all of the company's common stock – and thereby own the entire company – at the current stock market price. Of course, if anyone attempted to buy all the company's common stock in one instance, the forces of supply and demand would undoubtedly increase the current market value – or capitalization – of the stock.

The concept of capitalization will help us appreciate the ascendance of technology in the investment world.

In his book, ***The Four***, Scott Galloway listed the five largest capitalized U.S. companies in **2006**. Galloway then went on to list the five largest capitalized U.S. companies in **2019.** The following chart is notable not only in the total dominance of technology stocks in 2019, but also in the Market Capitalization numbers. Except for the inclusion of Microsoft in the **2006** rankings, every one of the 2019 entries had total capitalization amounts larger than every one of the 2006 entries.

The Ascendance of Technology Stocks		
Five Largest in 2006	*Market Capitalization*	*Market Cap March 2022*
Exxon Mobil	$540 Billion	$352 Billion
General Electric	$463 Billion	$103 Billion
Microsoft	$353 Billion	$2,251 Billion
Citigroup	$331 Billion	$111 Billion
Bank of America	$290 Billion	$348 Billion
Source: *The Four*, Scott Galloway, P. 7		*Yahoo!*
Six Largest in 2019	*Market Capitalization*	*Market Cap March 2022*
Microsoft	$905 Billion	$2,251 Billion
Apple	$896 Billion	$2,781 Billion
Amazon	$875 Billion	$1,660 Billion
Alphabet (Google)	$818 Billion	$1,830 Billion
Berkshire Hathaway	$494 Billion	$769 Billion
Meta Platforms (Facebook)	$476 Billion	$581 Billion
Source: *Wikipedia*		*Yahoo!*

Remember, the capitalization rate is computed by multiplying the shares outstanding by the current market price. Of those two components, the most variable is the current market value. In turn, as demonstrated in the following chart, it can be demonstrated that current market values are driven by actual and anticipated growth in revenues. As the following chart illustrates, the Tech Top 5 were increasing their revenues at a far greater rate than the largest capitalized companies of 2006.

Revenues Driving Stock Market Values

Largest in 2006	Revenues			Stock Market Values		
	2006	2019	% Change	2006	2019	% Change
Exxon Mobil	$377,635	$255,583	-32%	$56.42	$69.78	24%
General Electric	$163,391	$90,221	-45%	$270.00	$88.39	-67%
Microsoft	$44,282	$125,843	184%	$26.25	$257.70	882%
Citigroup	$146,558	$65,242	-55%	$490.00	$73.93	-85%
Bank of America	$117,017	$113,589	-3%	$46.92	$33.31	-29%
Source: Nasdaq				Source: Yahoo!		
Largest in 2019	2006	2019	% Change			
Microsoft	$44,282	$125,843	184%	$26.25	$257.70	882%
Apple	$19,315	$260,174	1247%	$2.59	$72.25	2690%
Amazon	$10,711	$280,522	2519%	$47.47	$1,847.84	3793%
Google	$23,651	$161,857	584%	$210.47	$1,337.02	535%
Facebook	$5,089	$70,697	1289%	$28.89	$205.25	610%
Source: Nasdaq				Source: Yahoo!		

Stock Market Values in the above chart were taken from the opening price in 2006 and the closing price in 2019. It should be noted that Google did not register annual revenues until 2009, and Facebook didn't until 2012.

To further exemplify the premise that revenue growth drives increasing stock market values, consider the performance of the following ten stocks.

It might be of interest for you to review these entries. How many of these companies are familiar to you? When you have finished reading this book you will almost certainly have the necessary information and tools to discover stocks with similar extraordinary growth potential. Each of these stocks was discovered using the screening metrics and research sources contained in this book and were made available to participants (Members} of my web site, *https://uvmetrics.com.*

Extraordinary Growth Stocks - Revenues Driving Stock Market Values

EGS Stars	Revenues			Stock Market Values		
	2019	2021	% Change	2019	2021	% Change
Advanced Micro Dev	$6,731,000	$16,434,000	144%	$18.01	$143.90	699%
Coupa Software	$389,000	$725,000	86%	$60.76	$158.05	160%
CrowdStrike	$481,000	$1,451,000	202%	$69.10	$204.75	196%
DataDog	$209,000	$1,028,000	392%	$34.25	$178.11	420%
MongoDB	$421,000	$873,000	107%	$81.40	$529.35	550%
Nvidia	$10,918,000	$26,914,000	147%	$32.66	$294.02	800%
Okta	$586,000	$1,300,000	122%	$61.10	$224.17	267%
Roku	$1,128,000	$2,764,000	145%	$29.82	$228.20	665%
SNAP	$1,715,000	$4,117,000	140%	$5.38	$47.03	774%
SiTime	$84,074	$218,808	160%	$17.50	$292.54	1572%
The Trade Desk	$661,000	$1,196,000	81%	$11.19	$91.64	719%
Source: Nasdaq				Source: Yahoo!		

Is the Digital Transformation a "Once and Done" Phenomena?

From an investment perspective, the digital transformation is just emerging. A lot of profits have already been made by perceptive investors. It's quite normal, therefore, to assume that the train has already left the station, that most of the potential profits available from the digital transformation have already been earned.

The following excerpts partially illustrate future opportunities for discovering companies with extraordinary revenue growth potential. Clearly, there will be more opportunities, many not yet known.

The following is taken from **Singularity University**, *Exponential Technology Trends That Will Define the Future*, September 13, 2021

Artificial Intelligence (AI) – *Companies have been hyping AI for many years, to the point where some organizational leaders have stopped paying attention. But AI is improving by leaps and bounds, and the data and the processing power that drive AI are becoming cheaper and easier to obtain – just a few reasons we're entering the age of AI.*

Augmented Reality and Virtual Reality (AR/VR) – *AR and VR are also technologies that might be underestimated as toys for entertainment and gaming. But these technologies are improving rapidly and finding use cases in medicine, architecture,* manufacturing, education, construction, and aerospace. In the near future expect to see more AR layered over your physical world.

Autonomous Vehicles – *A look at the A-list brands competing in this space – including Google, GM, Ford, Toyota, Tesla and Volkswagen – suggests a large potential market. The global market is expected to reach $65.3 billion by 2027. It's a huge financial opportunity, and the impact on our daily lives may be even more profound than the introduction of mass-produced autos a century ago.*

Blockchain – *If there were a "Transformative Technology of 2018" award to recognize potential to transform the global economy, blockchain would be a leading candidate. The potential to eliminate third parties from transactions is driving a global market for blockchain that's expected to grow 59% from 2016 to 2024.*

Data Science – *It's been said that data is the new oil in today's data economy, but that may be underestimating data's impact. Data will continue to be a key driver of the global economy going forward, and scarcity is not a concern. The outlook is also good for the future of work, as LinkedIn recently identified Data Scientist as one of the fastest growing jobs in the world.*

Biotech, Digital Biology – *Aging populations – and the interest in slowing or stopping the aging process altogether – is driving this sector. The ability to build human parts to replace failing organs and tissues or edit diseases out of our genomes is driving a biotech market that's estimated to be worth $727 billion by 2025 according to Grand View Research.*

Internet of Things (IoT) – *IoT is not just a global network of interconnected gadgets – with the rapidly expanding range of wearables and personal devices. IoT is all of us. The growing number of devices is expected to top 75 billion by 2025, according to Statista.*

3D Printing and Digital Fabrication – *3D printing is an exponential technology with disruptive potential far beyond what* *many people realize. Beyond transforming the way all products are designed, tested and prototyped, 3D printing may reinvent traditional manufacturing and supply chains as well – a $1.7 trillion opportunity according to Andre Wegner.*

Robotics – *Robots and drones are becoming more affordable, efficient, and collaborative, enabling the robotic industry to achieve unprecedented growth. Collaborative robots that work safely alongside humans, like the LoweBot that can monitor inventory and help customers locate products, are leading the way.*

Hopefully this chapter will provide you with the perspective that the digital transformation represents an extraordinary opportunity for investors, an opportunity that is just beginning.

More important, as you learn more and more about the digital transformation, your ***investment perspective*** will be strengthened.

Finally, the leading quote to this chapter is worth repeating:

"In terms of the internet, nothing has happened yet! The internet is still at the beginning of its beginning. It is only becoming. If we could climb into a time machine, journey 30 years into the future, and from that vantage look back to today, we'd realize that most of the greatest products running the lives of citizens in 2050 were not invented until after 2016."
The Inevitable, Kevin Kelly

Also, consider the first and last sentences from the article, *Top 10 Digital Transformation Trends For 2023* appearing in the October 10, 2022 issue of Forbes:

*"Digital transformation is **never** going to be done."*

*"2023 is setting up to be another fascinating year in technology and while markets continue to make us all a bit uneasy, it's all but certain technology is our **best path forward** as we seek to return to the next period of economic growth."*

Chapter 3 – Revenue Growth – the *Sine Qua Non* of ALL Research in the Age of Digital Transformation

"Don't gamble: take all your savings and buy some good stock and hold it till it goes up, then sell it. If it doesn't go up, don't buy it."

Will Rogers

The following was in an email received in August 2020, advertising a **Forbes** magazine sponsored webinar.

*"Make no mistake, we are in the middle of the biggest technology transformation in history. It has ushered in a radically different kind of market. One that has the capacity to not only improve lives but has also created an explosion of tech-driven **profit opportunities**.*

What lies ahead has the potential to create the greatest economic boom where real wealth is made, surpassing the period when we harnessed electricity, developed the magic of flight, or the invention of computers themselves.

We've been waiting for decades for an opportunity this big. How can you take advantage of it? How can you know which technologies truly transformational and which ones are illusory hypes that you should ignore?"

Of course, my answer to that rhetorical question is . . . ignore the Forbes webinar, just continue reading my book! However, I'm happy to have Forbes confirm one of the messages in my book. Namely, the *Digital Transformation* has arrived, and the investment opportunities are just beginning. And they are going to be *extraordinary!*

Most emerging growth companies follow an S-curve growth pattern, beginning with launch and eventually achieving maturity. The highest investment risk in that pattern is obviously just after launch. The highest investment returns are typically earned once a company gets beyond that early risk and before it becomes mature. That part of the curve is what my metrics have been designed to capture. Specifically, no company qualifies for an investment unless it achieves *at least 4 consecutive quarters with year-over-year revenue growth of at least 40% for each of those quarters* **and** *annualized revenues of at least $100 million.* Those two qualifiers ensure that a company has moved beyond the start-up phase and is following a strong upward trend in revenue growth. Over the years I have learned that there are ample opportunities for investors to discover and invest in these wealth building investments.

Keep in mind that the top line of every Income Statement is always **Revenues**. It's also important to keep in mind that these companies spend a lot of money to sustain their revenue growth and to capture their share of the potential market for their product or service. Therefore earnings – and particularly earnings per share, the conventional metric for assessing investment merits – are irrelevant when making investment decisions regarding high growth stocks.

There's a wonderful Warren Buffett quote that illustrates the importance of focusing on revenues:

"Writing a check separates commitment from conversation."

Revenues are generated by customers writing checks. That's why this book will lead you away from conversations – *opinions appearing in the financial media and blogs* – and enable you to laser focus on quarterly financial reports which illustrate commitments.

You may recall from Chapter 1 that early discoverers of market moving information – if they buy and **hold** their original investment – will almost always reap the largest profits from their investment. However, I went on to explain those early investments typically offer the greatest risk to investors. Furthermore, those early discoverers are seldom qualified to credibly analyze and determine a credible assessment of the future value for their investment. Consequently, faced with an unknown future and the allure significant early profits, the "greed/fear" cycle can compel early discoverers to sell too soon.

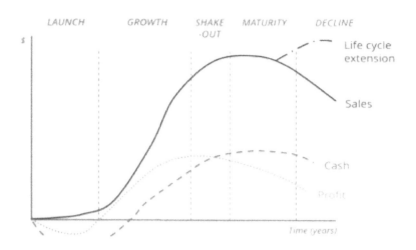

Revenue Growth – the *Sine Qua Non* of ALL Research

Although all three of my triggers are valuable in the discovery of tomorrow's winning stocks . . . *today*, the ***only indispensable*** trigger **is Revenue Growth.** If a company's revenue growth does not meet the minimum requirements of **four consecutive quarters of at least 40% year-over-year revenue growth** with **annualize revenues of at least $100 million,** no further research is performed for that company.

Source for Revenue Growth Data

I use *Briefing.com* as my principal source of percentage revenue growth data. It provides exactly what I'm looking for – percentage increase in year-over-year quarterly revenues. Before one can access this data, a subscription is required. My subscription – which was entered several years ago – costs **$67.50 per month** . . . and is worth every penny of that amount. As you will learn in subsequent chapters, *Briefing.com* is also a very valuable source of additional information that is both credible and timely.

Every day *Briefing.com* – in its *Calendar – Earnings Results* site – reports the quarterly results of every company reporting quarterly financial results for that day. All one must do is scan the *Yr to Yr Rev* column to detect companies that might qualify for the minimum requirement of 40% growth. That percentage can be flexible. As previously noted, my threshold for year-over-year revenue growth is 40% for at least one or more of the most recent four quarterly reports.

As you continue using the resources contained in this book you will become increasingly familiar with industries and companies. For example, when the Covid pandemic abated in early 2022, companies involved in travel, entertainment and food services experienced a strong recovery in revenues. Clearly these results were ephemeral and could be ignored.

Identifying the current quarterly results in *Briefing.com* is just the beginning in the revenue qualification process. Remember, I require one or more quarters of 40% or better year-over-year revenue growth.

So, where does one go to discover the 3-earlier quarters of revenue growth? There are several sources for that information, but I have found that the most expedient and the most credible source for that information is a company's home page.

To begin that process, go to *Yahoo* and enter the company's name or symbol in the *Search* box at the top of the page. Next, select *Profile* from the blue options in mid-page. Then select the blue URL for the company's web site. If an *Investors* or *Investor Relations* option is not apparent, scroll down to the bottom of that page where it almost always will be located. If a company does not have an *Investors* section, I would discontinue my research for that company.

Before going further, at this point you should create a Revenue Chart for this company. Since this chart will be updated with each quarterly financial report issued by the company, you will be using this chart for as long as you own this company's stock. This information will be your primary source for determining whether to hold – or sell – your investment. As mentioned in the *Introduction,* it should not be your only source for making that determination. The Quarterly Revenue chart template can be found in Chapter 6.

In the *Investors* category there should be a section entitled *Quarterly Results* with a user-friendly listing of current and previously released quarterly financial reports. Quite often these reports come in a variety of formats. The most useful option is the *News Release* issued by the corporation. At the bottom of this release, you will find an Income Statement which will provide *Revenues* for both the current and year ago quarter. **Both** should be entered in the Revenue Chart.

Continue that process for all four of the most recent quarters to determine if the company qualifies.

You will note that one of the columns is entitled *Forecast.* In almost all quarterly earnings releases issued by the corporation, there will be a section such as *Looking Ahead*, or *Next Quarter Estimate* and is usually located within the first three or four paragraphs of the News Release. This release should contain a revenue *forecast* for the next quarter that will be entered in the *Forecast* column of the Revenue Chart.

If there is no forecast for the next quarter, an alternative source might be in the *Quarterly Earnings Call Transcript*, usually found in *Seeking Alpha.* If a forecast number can't be found, you will not be able to track management's ability to forecast future revenues, but that does not have to be a showstopper.

A note of caution: Most companies *understate* this forecast. The reason for this understatement is that it reduces the possibility of *missing* their forecast, an eventuality that will cause analysts to lower their future projections, which usually results in increased selling pressure for the stock.

It's imperative that you create a new file or folder in your computer for every company that you invest in. Included in that file should be any research reports or other relevant sources of information that inspired you to invest in that company. The above Revenue Chart should also be uploaded to that company file. There will be times when your investment in that company will experience a downward trend in market value, whether caused by internal corporate developments or simply by overall market trends. At those times, you will find it very useful to review that folder to make a "Hold" or "Sell" decision.

Evaluating a company with no profits or earnings

Many of the high revenue growth companies that you will discover will not have profits or earnings, so conventional analytical metrics like *Price-to-earnings ratios* are simply not applicable. There is a new work-around metric that will help you determine the investment merits of these companies.

That metric is known as ***The Rule of 40***.

"The Rule of 40 is very helpful for assessing fundamental trade-offs between growth and profitability. Investors are often willing to tolerate low profits or net losses as long as a company is demonstrating strong growth. It's common for young companies to invest in growth by spending heavily on R&D or sales and marketing, even though those expenses will pinch profitability in the near term. The Rule of 40 was introduced to measure young, unproven companies. And that's where it really shines."

The Motley Fool

Here is the chart Template for creating The Rule of 40

					Revenue	Rule of
			Free Cash Flow / Rule of 40			
Company	Symbol	Revenues	Free Cash Flow	FCF %	Growth	40 Score

The Revenues column will be filled with the most recent quarter's Revenues. The Free Cash Flow can often be found in the corporate quarterly earnings release. If not there, it can be found in *Yahoo!*, but you will have to wait for that information to be updated by *Yahoo!* Or, if you're more familiar with the arcane world of corporate finance than I am, you can construct your own cash flow data from a company's *Income Statement.*

Once you have it, enter the Free Cash Flow in the appropriate space

To compute the FCF %, enter the following formula in Col E, Row 4:

=D4/C4

Enter the Revenue Growth percentage from the Revenue Chart.

To compute the *Rule of 40 Score,* enter the following formula in Col G, Row 4:

=F4+E4

Any score higher than 40 indicates that a company has met the *Rule of 40.*

After all of this, is the market price too high?

Market values can sometimes become unrealistically high, especially for companies that are considered to have extraordinary growth potential. Said differently, it's very possible to buy a stock that is priced too high, thereby diminishing the potential for higher future market values.

One of the most interesting metrics I've seen for determining a fair price to pay for a stock is *Discounted Cash Flow (DCF)*. Here's *Investopedia's* definition:

"Discounted cash flow (DCF) is a valuation method used to estimate the value of an investment based on its expected future cash flows. DCF analysis attempts to figure out the value of an investment today, based on projections of how much money it will generate in the future."

And here is their formula for computing DCF:

$$DCF=(CF_1/1 + r^1) + (CF_2/ 1 + r^2) + (CF_n /1 + r^n)$$

CF_1 is for year one,

CF_2 is for year two,

CF_n is for additional years

r = the discount rate

What DCF can tell you, from **Investopedia**:

"The purpose of DCF analysis is to estimate the money an investor would receive from an investment, adjusted for the time value of money. The time value of money assumes that a dollar today is worth more than a dollar tomorrow because it can be invested. As such, a DCF analysis is appropriate in any situation wherein a person is paying money in the present with expectations of receiving more money in the future.

For example, assuming a 5% annual interest rate, $1 in a savings account will be worth $1.05 in a year. Similarly, if a $1 payment is delayed for a year, its present value is 95 cents because you cannot transfer it to your savings account to earn interest."

And, again, from the estimable **John Bogle** . . . *"Sooner or later, the rewards of investing **must** be based on future cash flows. The purpose of any stock market, after all, is simply to provide liquidity for stocks in return for the promise of future cash flows, enabling* *investors to realize the present value of a future stream of income at any time.*"

For readers interested in learning more about *free cash flow,* I highly recommend **Expectations Investing** by Michael J. Mauboussin and Alfred Rappaport.

One final note on buying stocks at or shortly after their Initial Public Offering (IPO)

Some investment advisors and institutional investors will eschew investing in stocks that are being offered in their *Initial Public Offering.* The primary reason for this aversion relates to a concept know as *lock-up period.* Here's the way Wikipedia describes this concept:

"A lock-up period is a predetermined amount of time following an initial public offering where large shareholders, such as company executives and investors representing considerable ownership, are restricted from selling their shares.

The lockup period typically lasts between 90-180 days. Usually employees with options and early investors (venture capitalists) want shorter lockups (so they can cash out sooner) while the underwriting banks want longer lockups (to keep insiders from flooding the market and sinking the share price).

When lockup periods expire normal supply/demand metrics become unbalanced with the increased supply usually lowering market values. Therefore, some investors prefer to wait until the lockup period passes before making an investment. Of course, if the company's growth prospects are inordinately promising, those investors who defer buying the stock could eventually pay higher prices.

Thus far you have become familiar with the mechanics for discovering stocks with extraordinary growth potential. However, these "signals" represent just the beginning of the discovery process.

On their own, they are insufficient to develop the *perspective* you will need to make profitable investment decisions.

Chapter 4 – The Two Additional Discovery Triggers

"If calculus or algebra were required to be a great investor, I'd have to go back to delivering newspapers."

Warren Buffett

Each of these two *triggers* feature some of the most valuable and most certifiably accurate sources of investment information and are readily accessible by anyone. One of these sources is free while the other involves a modest annual or monthly fee.

To avoid confusion, throughout the three chapters of Discovery Triggers, the words *trigger* and *screen* are used interchangeably.

Either one of the two screens offers the potential to discover stocks with extraordinary stock market performance. Furthermore, as the word *discover* implies, it's very likely that you will discover these stocks *before* most investors. And each of the three screens is uncomplicated to implement. Although each screen can be used independently of the other, quite often the confluence of two of these screens heightens their efficacy.

Each screen illustrates the advantages that U.S. individual investors have over individual investors in most other countries. Those advantages are primarily found in the plethora of investment information that is available to U.S. investors, as well as in the accuracy and value of that information.

First, an explanation as to why screens are necessary.

EODData provides closing prices for a variety of exchanges in the US. A recent check of their listings revealed the following:

New York Stock Exchange – 3,504 listings

Nasdaq – 4,978 listings

American Stock Exchange – 2,684 listings

The total of those three entities comes to 11,166. I've seen estimates as high as 15,000. Therefore, pre-screening that universe is necessary simply to eliminate most companies that do not meet my investment requirements.

My Basic Guidelines That Apply to ALL Screens and ALL Research Sources

This is so important, it's worth repeating. If either of these two screens qualifies as an investment discovery, I urge you to forego making an investment decision unless a stock meets all the following required metrics:

Year over Year Quarterly Revenue Growth of at least 40% for the most recent four quarters. This metric offers proof that an increasing number of customers are buying the company's products or services.

Annualized Revenues of at least $100 million. Once this level of revenue has been attained, it illustrates that a company has advanced beyond the start-up stage, which quite often represents a higher risk level of failure in corporate evolution.

Significant Total Addressable Market (TAM). I want to be sure that a company's growth is not constrained by a finite, or limited, addressable market. Said differently, I want to have some confidence that extraordinary growth will be sustained moving into the future.

Unique Competitive Advantage (Moat). My revenue growth metrics offer evidence that some sort of moat does exist or that the TAM is large enough to sustain one or more competing entrants. However, there should be some evidence that a company's products or services offer a price and/or performance advantage over competing products or services. Knowing what problem(s) are solved by using a company's products or services helps to identify potential competitive advantages.

Management with proven successful performance in their fields of expertise. This is a key observation. A history of prior management successes suggests that the management team has a proven capability of driving extraordinary growth.

Most of the above information can be obtained from the company's home page. If not available there it almost certainly can be found in their Initial Public Offering (S-1) filing.

Many of the companies discovered by my metrics are in their early, not yet mature, stages of corporate growth as they as they rightly focus on increasing their market share (revenues), while profitability represents a future goal. A classical illustration of this focus was Amazon.com. Almost always, this is a period when most companies experience their largest percentage increase in revenues, as well as their **best** stock market performance.

Many of the companies discovered by these metrics are involved – either as customers or providers– in technologies immersed in the Digital Transformation.

The Unusual Percentage Increase in Price / Volume Screen

The rationale supporting this metric is very clear. When investors discover market moving information – new products, new markets, new management, etc. – two strong economic forces interact – the fundamental economic forces of Supply and Demand. The first is that an increasing number of investors want to own the stock resulting in increased Demand. The second is that investors who already own the stock become less willing to sell their stock, resulting in decreased Supply.

Since for every buyer there must be a seller, the only way that buyers can acquire the stock is to entice existing owners with higher stock market prices. As an increasing number of investors also discover the market moving information, the unusual percentage increases in both price and volume become more evident.

Fortunately, the dissemination of the market moving information is not instantaneous – there are no whistles blown or network news announcements. Like water trickling down a hillside, the discovery process is gradual, but nonetheless relentless.

This is how market price trends develop. The important observation is that all trends have a beginning, and therein lies the virtue of this price/volume metric. It enables alert investors to discover the beginning of important trends.

This trigger provides the timeliest information of most investment triggers. Price/Volume data is updated almost instantly throughout every trading day. However, for our purposes we are most concerned with end-of-day data.

Of the two values – Price and Volume – Price is obviously the most relevant since it's the only one of the two that reflects changing values. Volume, on the other hand, reflects the intensity of buying interest for that stock.

It's important to know that the closing price for most stocks rarely change more than 1% or 2% from one day to the next. Therefore, every incremental increase above those percentages reflects heightened demand for that stock. Said differently, more buyers (volume) are willing to pay higher prices to acquire the stock.

Once this metric identifies a stock that displays unusual percentage increases in Price and Volume, the challenge for all investors is to attempt to discover the market moving information that precipitated the percentage increases. This discovery process – and the perceptive interpretation of the market moving information – is what produces profitable investments.

There are several sources for Price/Volume data and – as might be expected – each involves a subscription fee. My preferred source is . . .

Barchart *(barchart.com)-* **Currently $29.95/month or $199.95/year.**

The subscription plan I use is called **Barchart Premier**.

Once in the Barchart home page, select **Stocks** (just below the barchart name at the top of the page).

In the pop-up section, select **Percent Change.**

Select the box – **Receive End-of-day Email**, then **Advances, All US Exchanges, Today** and **Main View.**

To the right of that line, select **Download.** An Excel icon will appear in the lower left corner of your computer. Select that icon to receive the Excel spreadsheet with all of that data.

After downloading the data, I make a few modifications to the Excel spreadsheet. The first step is to delete all of Row 1 (headings) to facilitate further sorting. Since we're primarily interested in percentage increases in Price and Volume, the **Change**, **High**, **Low** and **Time** columns can be deleted. You will now be left with Columns A – F.

You will note that there is no data available for the percentage chain in Volume. Therefore, in Row 1, Column G, enter the following formula:

=(E1-F1)/F1

Select all of Column G, go to **Number**, select **Percentage** and reset Decimal Places to 0.

I make one final modification to the spreadsheet and, although it is unrelated to percentage increases, I find it to be very useful since it reflects the apparent dollar volume related to each entry.

In Column H Row 2, enter the following formula:

=E2*C2

In the Excel **Numbers** option, I select *Currency* and *Dollars* and reduce the Decimal Places to zero.

Select Row 1, Columns G and H. Move your cursor to the lower right corner of Row 1, Column H. When a + sign appears, depress, and hold down, your right click mouse and drag your cursor down to the last data entry.

Once the above modifications have been completed, you can then sort the entries according to percentage increases in Price or Volume, or you can sort the entries to determine the apparent dollar volume related to each entry.

I sort the **Percent Change/Price** from highest to lowest and then delete any entries lower than 3%. I then sort the **Dollar Volume** (Col. G) from highest to lowest and then delete any entry lower than $1 million.

Why is that apparent dollar volume important? The higher the dollar volume, the more likely the percentage increases in Price and Volume were triggered by savvy institutional investors.

One of the virtues of the Excel spreadsheet is that the data can be sorted to reflect your area of interest. For example, the following can be sorted by any one of **the Percentage Change** or **Dollar Value** Columns.

One of the negatives of the Barchart daily emails is that they can't be accumulated. For example, if you miss processing the current day's email, that data will not be saved. Rather, the email will automatically update the data to reflect the data being generated by the current day's market activity.

An analysis of this data is seldom so compelling that I'm prepared to make a Buy decision. I want to know *why* the extraordinary percentage increases in Price and Volume occurred.

My first step is to visit *Yahoo!* to learn more about the company, and my initial interest is whether the company meets my Revenue requirements. Enter the company's symbol at the top of the *Yahoo!* site. Select **Financials**, **Income Statement**, then **Quarterly**. A quick glance will reveal whether the company might meet the revenue requirements. If it does, then follow the procedures disclosed in Chapter Four and construct a Revenue Chart. If it does not meet my revenue requirements, I do no further research for this company.

Another Way to Use Price/Volume Metrics – Using Affirm as an Illustration

I sometimes find it useful to determine if there have been *recent* percentage increases in Price/Volume – other than what has been discovered in the daily data provided by Barchart.

To access that information, I once again go to *Yahoo!* and select **Historic Data**.

Just below the blue **Apply** icon there is a selection for **Download**. Select that icon and an Excel spreadsheet will be downloaded to your computer with all of that data.

Place your cursor in Col A, Row !, select **All**, then select **Sort**, then select **Oldest to Newest**. I then delete Cols C, D, and F – the **High**, **Low** and **Adjusted Close** columns.\

I then enter my cursor in Col E, Row 20 and enter the following formula:

=average(D1:D20) and select **Enter**.

I then place my cursor in that square, move it to the lower-right corner until the cursor changes to a small +. While that is still evident, I depress and hold Left Click and drag the cursor down the entire data entry in Col E.

Next, in Col F Row 20 I enter the following formula:

=(D20-E20)/E20 and select *Enter*. I then select all of Col F, **Number**, **Percentage** with zero **Decimal Places**

I then place my cursor in that square, move it to the lower-right corner until the cursor changes to a small +. While that is still evident, I depress and hold Left Click and drag the cursor down the entire data entry in Col F.

I now have **Volume Percentage Increases** for all entries.

Next, place your cursor in Col G, Row 20 and enter the following formula:

=(C20-C19)/C19 and select *Enter*. I then select all of Col G, **Number**, **Percentage** with zero **Decimal Places**

I then place my cursor in that square, move it to the lower-right corner until the cursor changes to a small +. While that is still evident, I depress and hold Left Click and drag the cursor down the entire data entry in Col G.

I now have **Price Percentage Increases** for all entries.

Finally, in Col H, Row 240 I entered the following formula:

=D20*C20 and select **Enter**. I then select all of Col H, **Number**, **Currency** with zero **Decimal Places**

I then place my cursor in that square, move it to the lower-right corner until the cursor changes to a small +. While that is still evident, I depress and hold Left Click and drag the cursor down the entire data entry in Col H.

I now have potential **Currency** for all entries.

Scanning through those percentage increases I discovered the following metrics for Affirm:

	A	B	C	D	E	F	G
		Affirm (AFRM) - Price/Volume Signals					
2		Price Data		Volume Data			
3	Date	Close	% Change	Today	Average	% Change	$ Volume
4	16-Mar-22	33.34	18%	18,707,700	12,587,060	49%	$62,371,718
5	17-Mar-22	36.75	10%	15,254,700	12,581,600	21%	$560,610,225
6	18-Mar-22	40.71	11%	20,081,900	12,513,590	60%	$817,534,149
7							$1,440,516,092

The conclusion that might be drawn from this data is that almost **$1.5 billion** was invested in Affirm over a three-day period. That level of dollar volume almost certainly represented aggressive buying by one or more institutional investors. In addition, both the Price and Volume percentage increases were extraordinary, suggesting that these investors were convinced that AFRM's closing prices offered extraordinary profit potential.

This chart also illustrates the benefit of combining three or more days in constructing one's Price/Volume daily chart.

If an investor already owned AFRM, that data might encourage him or her to maintain or increase their holdings. It might also encourage non-owners of AFRM to consider making an investment in AFRM.

The SEC Filings Trigger -

"We don't think it's appropriate to arm some people with slingshots and send them into battle with people armed with laser-guided missiles."

Jay Kemp Smith, Chairman, Leading Market Technologies

The ultimate quest for both the folks with slingshots and the folks armed with laser-guided missiles is to become an early discoverer of market moving information.

Given the vast resources at their disposal to acquire and analyze market moving information, institutional investors are clearly the folks with the laser-guided missiles. Collectively they literally spend **billions** of dollars every year for investment research.

To ensure that individual investors are not disadvantaged in the competitive world of investing, institutional investors must comply with filing requirements mandated by the Securities and Exchange Commission (SEC). The essential purpose of these filings is to provide transparency regarding the investment activities of institutional investors, as well as publicly owned corporations.

There are several unique values for individual investors stemming from these filing requirements. First, they are free to all investors. Second, because of the potential penalties for false or misleading information, the authenticity of that information is **certifiable**. The third value is that all these documents are easily accessible on the Internet for all investors.

The following is a brief description of some of the more pertinent Security and Exchange Commission (SEC) filing requirements.

Filing requirements for corporations

S-1 – Any corporation seeking to enter the domain of publicly traded stocks must file this report prior to being listed on any of the nation's stock exchanges where *all* publicly owned stocks are traded. This is probably the most comprehensive and most reliable source of information available to investors. This report is known as the Initial Public Offering (IPO) document.

10-K – Applies to all companies whose stock is publicly traded. Provides a comprehensive overview of the company's business and financial condition for the past year. Must be filed within 60-days of the end of a fiscal year. This report also contains financial data for the fourth quarter.

10-Q - Applies to all companies whose stock is publicly traded. Provides a comprehensive overview of the company's business and financial condition for the latest quarter. Must be filed within 40-days of the end of each quarter.

There are two locations where the above filings can be found. The first is the company's website. When there, select **Investor Relations**. Most informed companies will have a section entitled **SEC Filings**. The second option can be found at https://www.nasdaq.com/. This location has lots of very useful investing information. To get started, enter the name of the company or its stock symbol in the white box along the right edge and select *Enter* on your computer. Note that there is a list of options on the left side of this site, some of which you will refer to in the future. For now, just select **SEC Filings**.

Filing requirements for institutional investors

SC- 13G – Institutional investment managers are required to file within 45 days of the end of the year in which they finish above 5%, or within 10 days of first finishing a month above 10%.

13F-HR – Any institutional investment manager with a total market value of at least $100,000,000 must file a report listing all their individual stock investments within 45 days after the last day of each calendar year and within 45 days after the last day of each of the first three calendar quarters of the subsequent calendar year.

Most institutional investor stock holdings are so large and so varied that their stock holdings are essentially a proxy for the overall market. However, if they all owned the same overall percentages of the same core stocks their performances would be very similar. Said differently, none would have a competitive performance advantage. However, since the earnings of every one of those firms are determined by the level of assets that they manage – the more assets they manage, the more money they earn – they all strive for a competitive performance advantage since better performance will almost always attract more assets for the firm to manage.

Institutional investment managers know that to perform better than their peers, they must discover market moving investment information *before* that information has become widely disseminated.

When institutional and hedge fund managers discover market moving information regarding a specific stock, they do what any savvy investor would do – they make a significant purchase of that stock. For institutional investors a *significant* purchase typically means buying hundreds of thousands – or millions – of shares. In the parlance of Wall Street, they make **Big Bets**.

Often those big bets involve acquiring *five percent* or more of a company's issued and outstanding common stock. That triggers the requirement for an SC 13-G filing. Those filings are listed every day at the following URL:

https://www.sec.gov/cgi-bin/browse-edgar?company=&CIK=&type=SC+13G&owner=include&count=40&action=getcurrent

Once that original SC-13G filing has been sent to the SEC, any changes to that original or most recent filing – either an increase or a decrease in the number of shares owned – triggers the requirement for an amendment to the original (SC-13G) or most recent (SC-13G/A) filing.

Although this information is free, it's probably the most difficult of my three discovery sources to use. There are several reasons for the diminished value of the 13-G information.

The first disadvantage is the plethora of these filings, particularly during the first quarter of each calendar year when institutional investment management firms, hedge funds and mutual funds reflect year-end changes or adjustments to their portfolios. It is almost impossible for an individual investor to analyze the tsunami of these first quarter filings.

Another disadvantage is the fact that institutional investors can endure losing investments with less discomfort than individual investors. The reason for this is their huge base of investments. One bad investment has an insignificant impact on their overall performance. For that reason, institutional investors can afford to take chances that most individual investors would be foolish to take. Offsetting that risk, most institutional investors know that the best investment returns often are gained by investing in stocks with a high level or risk that have been carefully and thoroughly analyzed to mitigate that risk.

A further, albeit minor, disadvantage is the timing of the 13-G reports. Remember that institutional investors have 45-days to meet the requirements of a 13-G or 13G/A filing. This is a minor disadvantage since most stocks require time to develop strong upward trends in market values. More important, the investment horizon for institutional investors is typically measured in years, not days or months. That extended horizon offers individual investors ample time to invest in stocks being bought by institutional investors – provided those investments meet the Basic Requirements mentioned in the Chapter 3.

I tracked the flow of SC-13G and 13-G/A filings for several years and the overall results were nonplus. I could discern no value in this methodology since the overall gains and losses were often equally balanced.

Having said that, I have learned that some institutional investors have reasonably reliable track records regarding their 13-G and 13-G/A filings. For example, I have found that Fidelity Funds *(listed as FMR)* – which report their 13-G filings on the 10th of *every* month – can periodically produce investment gems. What I have found to be of investment value is when Fidelity – or any other institutional investor – reveals that they have acquired significantly more than the basic, required 5% ownership.

If you are reading this online, the following links will connect you to 13-G filings that I follow on a regular basis:

Fidelity Funds

T Rowe Price

State Street

Morgan Stanley

Renaissance Technologies

JPMorgan Chase

How can you identify 13-G filers that might be worth following?

A quick answer to that question is to look for the companies being bought. In the listing of 13-G filings, they are identified as either *Filed by* or *Subject*. The latter identifies the company whose stock is being bought. If you are familiar with that company or know that it's in an industry that is experiencing above-average growth – such as semiconductors in late 2021 and early 2022 – that could trigger your interest to pursue further due diligence.

There is a very significant benefit within the SC-13G category that can be obtained by individual investors. That benefit relates to follow-on SC-13G/A filings and can be used by individual investors for both Buy and Sell decisions.

Let's first look at the benefit related to Sell decisions. This benefit will have value primarily if one already owns the stock in the filing. When a SC-13G/A filing reflects a reduction or an elimination of shares owned by an institutional investor, that would normally be a negative signal. Of course, as with individual investors, there can be many reasons why a stock is being sold by an institutional investor. Nevertheless, one can reasonably assume that such a filing is *not* a positive.

Unfortunately, with one exception, the SC-13G/A filing does not inform an investor if the filing is an increase or a decrease in the number of shares owned. That one exception can be found in **Item 5** of the filing – *Ownership of five percent or less of a class*. If there is an **(X)** at the end of that entry, then the filer no longer owns five percent of the stock, the consequence of a recent sale by the filer.

So, how does one determine whether the SC-13G/A filing represents an increase of a decrease in the number of shares owned if the Item 5 is not checked? The answer can be found in a 13F-HR filing which lists all the stocks owned by the institutional filer.

The first step is to record the number of shares listed in the SC-13G/A filing.

As noted above, 13F-HR documents are filed quarterly so it's important to retrieve the most recent filing. To find these filings, return to the original site listing the daily SC-13G filings/ Instead of selecting the *Subject*, select the *Filed by* entry. The resulting site may or may not have a 13F-HR entry. If it does, select the **most recent**. If it does not, enter **13F-HR** in the **Filing Type** in the upper left corner. Then, to the right, select *Search*. Typically, there will be four or five options to choose from to access the listing of stocks. You will want the option that lists, in alphabetical order, all the stocks owned by the filer as of the filing date.

By comparing the number of shares in the SC-13G/A with the number of shares in the most recent 13F-HR filing, one can easily determine whether the SC-13G/A was an increase or decrease in ownership.

One final note. All the filing requirements of SC-13G and SC-13G/A also apply to individual investors when their ownership of a particular stock crosses the 5% threshold.

Finding information to meet the final three investment requirements

Chapter Three provided solutions for meeting the first two of my investment requirements. However, thus far I have not provided solutions for meeting the final three investment requirements. Specifically . . .

Significant Total Addressable Market (TAM).

Unique Competitive Advantage (Moat).

Management with proven successful performance

The most comprehensive source of information regarding these guidelines can be found in one source – a company's **S-1 filing** – their Initial Public Offering (IPO) document. Many of the companies that you will be researching are in the early stages of their business cycle. Most corporations have – in the *Investor Relations* section of their Home web site – a listing of SEC Filings which should include the S-1 filing. Also, as previously mentioned, S-1 filings can be found in the *Nasdaq* site under **SEC Filings.**

S-1 filings are extraordinarily comprehensive and will usually provide information regarding all three of the above requirements.

Chapter 5 – Acquiring Perspective

Before explaining the meaning of perspective as it relates to investing and before showing you how to acquire it, let me first explain why perspective is **essential** and why it will help you to become a smarter, more successful investor.

Perspective will enable you to avoid the two most damaging forces that prevent many investors from being more successful. Those forces are **fear** and **greed.** Markets and specific investments will always fluctuate and, often, those fluctuations are activated and sustained by fear and/or greed. Neither fear nor greed represents rational, deliberate decision making. It is perhaps normal for individuals to experience fear when markets or an investment decline in value – the awful sense that one's wealth is declining is clearly emotional and not rational. Similarly, many investors experience greed when markets or an individual investment appreciates in value – the delightful sense that one's wealth is appreciating is also clearly emotional and not rational. When investors are guided by fear and greed there is tendency to buy high and sell low, which is just the antithesis of the exemplary mantra for successful investing . . . buy low and sell high,

In the Introduction I related the fictional experience that Harry Brown had with his Nvidia investment. Harry's investment experience with NVDA displayed **perspective.** Fear was not part of his decision making because he had done his homework. His decisions to be patient and not sell when bad news and declining market values caused many Nvidia investors to join the selling stampede and "bail out" were rational. As it turned out, Harry was ultimately richly rewarded for his perspective. He was an intelligent, not an emotional, investor. He did his homework by reading company reports and letting the good news – not the bad news – dominate his thinking.

Sources for Acquiring Perspective

As the following will illustrate, there are no shortcuts to acquiring perspective. You, as an investor, can do as much or as little as you opt to do. Obviously, the more knowledge you acquire about a specific investment opportunity, the more perspective you will have.

Some of the following sources will require either a monthly or annual subscription. I will also include sources that are free. Many of the sources requiring a subscription do offer a free trial period, enabling you to assess the value of the investment information provided.

Let's begin with the sources requiring a subscription. I will not mention the required fee for subscription since that number can – and does – change. The required fee can be found on the website of each source. The URL for each website is listed after the name.

Seeking Alpha - https://seekingalpha.com

There are several reasons why I listed this source at the beginning.

First, *Seeking Alpha* is the source for one of the most important sources of investment information available to individual investors. I'm referring to the **Quarterly Earnings Conference Call** transcription which can be found under NEWS. These conference calls are hosted by C-level executives, and the principal host is usually the CEO. They are offered primarily to provide information to research analysts regarding the company's performance during the most recent quarter. Analysts typically participate telephonically. In addition to the company's presentation, there is always a Q&A session at the end of the transcript in which analysts are invited to pose questions to the company's management.

Second, *Seeking Alpha* enabled me to discover many research providers that I subsequently subscribed to. The content for this site is largely provided by independent – typically non-Wall Street – research sources. As a subscriber, you will have the opportunity to receive free research reports from those independent researchers. Whenever you opt to **Follow** a particular researcher, every new report they publish will automatically sent to your email. Some will be good, others not so good. Over time you will be able to discern the difference. One of the interesting features is that you can opt to **follow** analysts who impress you with their research. You may ultimately opt to subscribe to the off-site service provided by some of these researchers. Also, when I want to learn more about a specific company, I will visit *Seeking Alpha*, enter the company name and review some of the research reports – found under **Analysis** - written about the company. Whether the reports are positive or negative, I almost always learn something from these reports.

Third, also under NEWS, you will find a compilation of relevant news from a wide range of news sources. This information will obviously deepen your perspective.

The following two sites are basic requirements for any individual investor:

Briefing.com – As previously noted, Briefing.com can be accessed only through a subscription. The Quarterly Revenue information provided by Briefing.com was covered in Chapter 4. There is another feature that is of equal value. Select **Portfolios & Emails** and enter all of the stocks that you want to follow. Any relevant news that Briefing.com might unearth will be automatically sent to your email, including comments and **Price Targets** from analysts working for Wall Street firms.

Yahoo! –Most of you will be familiar with Yahoo. I'm including it here for two reasons. First, select **My Portfolio** and enter stocks that you own and/or want to track. I use this service for creating *Monthly Valuation* charts. This feature is also a very convenient way to periodically check the valuations of your stocks, as well as the popular averages, which are listed at the top of this page. Instead of looking up values for individual stocks, just select **Export** on the right side of the line **My Portfolios.** All your stocks will be downloaded in Excel format which can be copied and pasted into your Monthly Valuation chart. Second, I always go to Yahoo! when I want to find the website for a stock of interest. After you've entered the stock symbol, select **Profile**. The stock's website will be listed under the company's address.

Subscription Sources

The following top three are my choices for both market and specific stock research. Just select each URL to learn more about their research. Each requires a subscription.

Beth Kindig – https://seekingalpha.com/author/beth-kindig

CML Pro – https://pro.cmlviz.com/getting-started-with-cml-pro/

Bert Hochfeld – https://seekingalpha.com/author/bert-hochfeld

The Information – https://www.theinformation.com – These folks consider themselves to be the Wall Street Journal on the West Coast. And, yes, they are that good.

MIT Technology Review – https://www.technologyreview.com

Free Sources

The Technology Letter - https://www.thetechnologyletter.com/ - This is an extraordinarily good source of investment ideas, particularly those relating to the Digital Transformation. Remarkably, it is FREE. It is written by Tiernan Ray, formerly the chief technology writer for *Forbes* magazine, and is published at least weekly. Quite often the articles feature interviews with CEOs of companies being featured, and therein lies the reason why it is free. My guess is that the companies pay Tiernan. I want to emphasize that this is only a guess, since we all know . . . here are no free lunches. Whether true or not, the fact remains that this is an extraordinarily good source of investment information.

Silicon Investor - https://www.siliconinvestor.com/ - *"Silicon Investor is the first website that evaluated the stocks of high-tech companies. It is an Internet forum and social networking service concentrating on stock market discussion, with particular focus on tech stocks."* Wikipedia. It is more popularly known as a "chat group", most of which are of questionable value. That is not an apt description of Silicon Investor, which features some of the most knowledgeable, sophisticated sharing of technology analyses on the Internet. As with most other sources of investment information, you will have to pick and choose the "threads" you find to be of value and interest.

YouTube - https://www.youtube.com/ - When you land on the Home page, you can simply surf through the choices offered, searching for sources that relate to the market or individual stocks. I haven't used YouTube very much, but the times that I have used it resulted in acquiring very good information. In the **Search** box at the top of the page, enter the company's *Symbol* or *Name*. Most progressive companies – those that view potential investors as an asset – are very proactive in providing videos that explain their product or service competitive advantages.

Ark Invest - https://ark-invest.com/subscribe/ - *"Investing in innovation starts with understanding it. ARK publishes its original research to enlighten investors on the impact of technologies and to seek feedback on our work."* I've always wondered why more institutional investors – including hedge funds – failed to share the research supporting their investment decisions with all investors. After all, if they share that research – and if it's convincing – wouldn't that increase the *demand* for their stock picks and perhaps increase the market value of those picks? ARK is particularly focused on companies with technologies that disrupt. ARK provides selected tidbits on a few of their picks, every Monday. To receive those free emails, just enter your information in this website.

As you immerse yourself in frequent visits to these websites, you will discover other sources of investment information that will be provided by the authors posting their research on these sites. The ultimate consequence of this immersion will be a significant increase in your **perspective.**

According to Ophir Gottlieb, *"Investors with perspective are the best investors in the world."*

Chapter 6 – Getting Started

"Wall Street is the only place that people ride to in a Rolls-Royce to get advice from those who take the subway."
Warren Buffet

Having read this far, hopefully you've acquired a lot of useful investing information. Using one of my three discovery metrics you've learned how to discover stocks with the potential to increase your wealth.

Or perhaps you have read an article or heard from relatives or friends about a stock that has piqued your interest.

Your obvious question might be, "How can I properly analyze this stock to determine if it deserves a place in my portfolio?". And, "How do I begin that process?".

There might be several viable steps that you can take. But, since you're reading my book, let me tell you the steps that I take in analyzing stocks that have piqued my interest.

Once a stock of interest has been identified, I go to *Yahoo!* Finance and enter either the name or the symbol of that stock. Of course, the first item I notice is the current market value and the 52-week price range. If the current price is closer to it's 52-week low than to it's high, I will want to learn why. I then select the **Profile** option and check where the company is headquartered. I tend to be partial to U.S. locations. I then check Sector and Industry. Since my investment focus is on the Digital Transformation, I want to determine that the company fits within that category. While still in *Yahoo!*, I quickly check **Financials/Income Statement/Annual.** I want to be sure that the company qualifies for the $100 million in annual revenue. That determination can be made by simply looking at the **TTM** listing. I then return to **Profile** and select the company's web site which is located directly below their phone number.

Upon entering the web site, I want to locate **Investors** or **Investor Relations** which is typically found under **Company**. If I have a problem locating *investors,* I scroll down to the bottom of the web site to find all the pages for this web site. If I can't find *Investors* and I am convinced that it just doesn't exist, I stop my search, and move on to another stock. Any company that does not have an *Investors* section is inarguably remiss in communicating with its owners – their investors.

When I do find the *Investors* section, I look for **Quarterly Results** which may be a separate item in *Investors* or else located under *Finances.* At this point I will want to retrieve my **Quarterly Revenue Growth Template**. Chapter 7 will show you how to populate data in this chart. I will often be offered several formats for the retrieval of this information. I always prefer to use the **Earnings Release** format since it contains all the information I will need for the Chart. Remember, what I'm looking for is four consecutive quarters with revenue growth of more than 40%. You might opt for whatever percentage increase you might deem to be more appropriate.

There are two additional steps that can be taken to confirm or disapprove my decision to buy this stock. Both metrics for performing this step are provided in Chapter 7.

The first step is to determine that there is no recent evidence of a *negative price trend* developing as evidenced by unusual percentage increases in Volume accompanied by unusual percentage decreases in Price. Of course, the antithesis – recent evidence of a *positive price trend* developing as evidenced by unusual percentage increases in Volume accompanied by unusual percentage increases in Price – would be a welcome discovery.

Next, I take a quick visit to *Nasdaq/Institutional Investors* to determine if institutional investors have – on balance – been buyers or sellers of the stock.

Thus far, I have completed the *quantitative analysis* for this stock. Next I want to complete the *qualitative analysis* – which is the analysis that will provide me with **perspective.**

My first qualitative visit is to **Seeking Alpha.** I will review at least two Research Reports found under *Analysis*, hopefully one positive and one negative to provide a balanced view. I will then read **all** of the most recent **Quarterly Earnings Call Transcript**, found under the *News* heading. I am particularly interested in the Q&A section at the end of this report. This is a particularly informative document. It provides the company with an opportunity to explain the "how and why" of their performance for the just ended quarter. Adding emphasis to the importance and the credibility of this document is that the target audience consists of Wall Street analysts. The two principal corporate presenters are usually the CEO and the CFO.

Chapter 7 – Knowing When to Sell

For most investors, deciding when to sell a stock is more difficult than deciding when to buy. This book has provided some proven sources and metrics to help with your decisions to buy specific stocks.

This chapter will provide you with sources and metrics to help with your decisions to sell specific stocks.

Many of the sources of information for this chapter have been identified in previous chapters. What's new about this chapter are the charts that will be used for entering and analyzing that information.

Quarterly Revenue Growth

You have perhaps already developed this chart for each of the stocks that you own. Of course, the key data to observe is whether the quarterly revenue data is increasing or decreasing. If the former, there perhaps will be no reason for you to consider selling the stock.

If the latter, you first retrieve your *folder* for this stock and review the research that provided your reasons for buying. You might also want to review the Quarterly Earnings Transcript in *Seeking Alpha* along with the company's Quarterly Earnings Release to learn if the company has provided a reasonable explanation for the decline in revenues. When you visit the *Seeking* Alpha site, review some of the recent *Research Reports* and *News* to learn of any negatives regarding the company's prospects.

There is another reason why you might choose to sell a stock, even if the revenue growth rate has been sustained. There will be instances when you discover a stock with compelling reasons to purchase but you don't have the funds to make that purchase. One of the ways to generate the funds to make a new investment is to sell one of your existing holdings. To help with the decision as to which of your existing investments to sell can be facilitated with the following chart – which should be completed during every quarterly earnings season.

					EGS 2022Q3 Y-O-Y Revenue Growth						
				Latest 4-Quarters					2022Q3		2022Q4
Company	Symbol	Report Date	2021Q4	2022Q1	2022Q2	2022Q3	Average	Forecast	Actual	Diff	Forecast

All the data for this chart can be found in the charts that you have already created for the individual stocks that you own. There are just two formulae that must be entered.

In Column H, Row 4, entered the following formula:

=average(G4:D4)

Copy that formula down through all the entries in Column H.

In Column K, Row 4, entered the following formula:

=J4-I4

Copy that formula down through all the entries in Column K.

There are just two numbers that I will consider once this chart has been completed.

First, the difference between Forecast and Actual. This number reveals the ability of management to accurately forecast and is particularly important if the number is negative.

Second, management's forecast for the next quarter (final column). This number reveals whether or not the revenue growth rate of previous quarters will be sustained.

The virtue of this chart is that it provides an overview of **all** the stocks in your portfolio, enabling you to decide which is the best candidate for sale.

13G and 13G/A SEC Filings

The best source for this information, and probably the most reliable and expeditious, is *Nasdaq* . . . *https://www.nasdaq.com/market-activity/stocks*.

In the large, black area, enter the stock *Symbol.*

On the new page, in the drop-down menu on the left, select *Institutional Holdings.*

There's a lot of valuable data on this site. Scroll down to *New and Sold Out Positions* and then scroll down to the different data categories, beginning with *Total.*

Select the *Total* heading. This category is undoubtedly the most important. It shows the largest institutional owners of a company's stock and the percentage *Change* in those holdings as reported by each institution's most recent quarterly **13F-HR** filing.

I would also select the *New, Increased, Decreased* and *Sold Out* columns.

In a sense, institutional investors – large as they are – often have the same problem of insufficient funds when they decide to add a new position to their portfolio. Therefore, selling portions of an existing position represents a source of funds. However, when the percentage change advances beyond a *negative 10%,* my concern for that stock grows.

On the other hand, when the percentage change advances beyond a *positive 10%,* my conviction for that stock grows.

Unusual Percentage Increases in Price and Volume

Generating this information is not as simple as the previous two sources. Once you've become familiar with the process of generating useful data, it might take 15 minutes for each stock that you analyze.

The virtue of this analysis is that it's very timely whereas the previous two methods rely on historic data that doesn't offer the benefit of timeliness.

The source for the data required for this metric is *Yahoo!* The URL is https://finance.yahoo.com/.

Enter the symbol for the stock at the top of the page. When the site for the stock appears, select *Historical Data* from the options in mid-page. Just above all the data select *Download.* Select the icon for that file which will appear in the lower left section of your computer. The Excel file will then appear on your computer screen.

You will not need all that data, so let's remove some of the unnecessary data.

Delete all of Columns C, D, and F.

Delete Row 1.

Place your cursor in Column A. Row 1.

On your keyboard, press and hold *Ctrl A*

Right Click with your cursor, then select *Sort* from the drop-down menu, then select *Oldest to Newest.*

In Column F, Row 20, enter the following formula:

=AVERAGE(E1:E20), then select *Enter* on your keyboard.

In Column G, Row 20, enter the following formula:

=(E20-F20)/F20, then select *Enter* on your keyboard.

Select all of Column G, then *Number,* then *Percentage*, then *0 Decimal Places.*

In Column H, Row 20, enter the following formula:

=(C20-C19)/C19, then select *Enter* on your keyboard.

Select all of Column H, then *Number,* then *Percentage,* then *0 Decimal Places.*

Select Row 20, Columns F, G and H. Depress and hold your cursor in the lower right corner of Row20, Column H until a + sign appears. Drag your cursor down through all remaining data in Columns G and H.

At this point, you have generated percentage increases for both Price and Volume. However, you're only interested in **recent** data, so scroll down to the most recent data entries.

Remember that percentage Price decreases are rarely more than plus or minus 2%. Therefore, you will be looking for *Price decreases greater than minus 2%*, accompanied by *Volume increases* – I would suggest – *greater than 10%.*

Chapter 8 – Organizing Your Research and Monitoring Performance

"One thing that could help would be to write down the reason you are buying a stock before you purchase. Write down 'I am buying Microsoft at $300 billion because . . . '. Force yourself to write this down. It clarifies your mind and discipline."
Warren Buffet

Organizing Your Research

During your search for investment candidates, you will acquire a lot of information, including research reports, analyst's research and target prices *(from Briefing.com)* and your own Excel Revenue Charts. As you access information relevant to your research, I would encourage you to copy and paste as much of that source information into a Word document. Give each document a relevant title beginning with the entry date to facilitate recall. Create a folder on your computer and name it something like *"Why I Invested in Nvidia"* and save your documents in the new folder. You might place that folder inside a larger folder entitled *"My Investments"*.

As mentioned in an earlier chapter, whether caused by overall market trends or by specific news related to one or more of stocks you've included in your portfolio, the value of your investments will fluctuate. I have learned that keeping, updating and reviewing the information filed in my individual stock folders can be very helpful when declining market values trigger the *fear* factor and I have to decide whether to sell, buy more to lower my average cost or . . . do nothing. By reviewing your saved files, such decisions are simplified, and the emotion of fear vanishes.

Monitoring Performance

Failing to measure your investment performance is sort of like competing in an athletic event without keeping score. Perhaps some of you can remember one of the famous quotes from former Green Bay Packers coach Vince Lombardi. An aggressive reporter was interviewing Coach Lombardi and asked the coach why he was so competitive. To prove his point the reporter recited the final two lines in one of the many poems written about sports by America's renowned sportswriter, Grantland Rice.

"For when the One Great Scorer comes to mark against your name, it matters not that you won or lost, but how you played the Game."

To which Lombardi succinctly replied, *"Then why do they keep score!"*

Of course, there is a huge difference between keeping score in athletic competitions and keeping score with your investment performance. The former is all about pride, trophies, championships, and ego padding. Monitoring performance provides investors with a clear picture about how effectively their wealth is being increased – or decreased. In the world of investing, *how you played the game* determines whether your wealth is being increased or decreased.

Unless investing is something other than an effort to increase one's wealth – perhaps an educational or avocational pursuit – keeping score ought to be an indispensable requirement for every individual investor.

Monitoring templates

There are several Templates that can be used in the monitoring process. The following are the templates that I use. Although I've used these templates specifically for portfolios relating to stocks involved with the Digital Transformation, there is no reason why they can't be used for **all** portfolios – including those being managed by an investment management firm that you have hired.

Cash Flow Chart

This is the foundation document for monitoring performance. It is also a significant source for Income Tax preparation.

Date	Action	Company	Symbol	Shares	Price	Cost	Proceeds	Cash

Your first entry – the beginning dollar amount to launch your portfolio – should appear in Row 3, Column I.

There are three formulas that should be entered in this chart.

For BUY transactions, enter the following formula in **Column G** and in subsequent Rows containing BUY transactions: _(I've entered Row numbers for illustration purposes. Use the appropriate Row number for actual transactions.)_

=E3*F3

For SELL transactions, enter the following formula in **Column H** and in subsequent Rows containing SELL transactions:

=E3*F3

In Column I, Row 4, enter the following formula:

=(I3-G4+H4)

Note: It will not be necessary to repeatedly enter these formulae for every transaction.

If the new entry is a **Buy**, simply go to the most recent Buy in **Column G**, select that cell, Select **Copy,** place your cursor in Column G associated with the new Buy and select **Paste.**

If the new entry is a **Sell**, simply go to the most recent Buy in **Column H**, select that cell, Select **Copy,** place your cursor in Column H associated with the new Sell and select **Paste.**

ALL entries – Buy and Sell – in Column I can be copied and pasted from the original entry in Column I.

Monthly Performance Chart

Although this is labeled as MONTHLY, you can change the frequency to whatever time span you prefer. Most investment management firms just issue quarterly reports. This template can be used to find a SELL candidate to be replaced by a new BUY candidate, simply by ranking the *% Change* column. The theory is, if you find a stock with better potential than your current worst performing stock, make the trade.

				MONTHLY Valuation				
				Entry Data			March 9, 2022	
Company	Symbol	Date	# Shares	Per Share	Cost	Per Share	Value	% Change

www.finance.yahoo.com/portfolios

You have to be careful to update your holdings in the *Yahoo!* site as you make changes to your portfolio. Once your portfolio is active, enter your initial stocks in the *Yahoo!* site. When you are ready to create a valuation update, select the *Export* option in the upper right corner. An icon should appear in the lower left corner of your computer screen containing – in *Excel* format – a lot of information relative to your portfolio. I use the *Paint Brush* option in *Excel* to capture the format of one of the numbers in Column G, then copy that format to all the price valuations in the *Yahoo!* spreadsheet and then copy that entire column and paste it to Row 4 of Column G.

In Column H, Row 4, enter the following formula:

=G4*D4

In Column I, Row 4, enter the following formula:

=(H4-F4)/F4

Quarterly Revenue Chart There are several sources for quarterly revenue data. The best, most reliable source is a company's *Home* page. Go to the *Investor Relations* site and select *Financial Information* and then, *Quarterly Financials.* Look for and select the article announcing the most recent quarterly financial results. There might be several sources offered for the retrieval of that information. The source that I use is the *Press Release.* It contains all the information that I want to retrieve.

The *first* data reference you might want to capture is the company's *Forecast* revenues and earnings for the *next* quarterly earnings report. This information is also usually listed in the beginning of the press release.

The *second* data reference you will need is usually at the end of the report – *Revenues.* This chart will almost always contain the current quarter's revenues as well as the year-ago quarter's revenues, i.e., 2021Q1 and 2022Q1. If you don't already have the previous year's revenues, enter that data as well as the current quarter's data.

If you are just starting this file for a company and need data from previous quarters/years, most enlightened companies will offer user-friendly data from previous years. They will also offer that information in different formats. I always select the *Press Release* format.

		Company (Symbol)				
		Quarterly Revenue Analysis				
FY		Report Date	Forecast	Forecast Y/Y Change	Actual	Actual Y/Y Change
2021	Q1					
	Q2					
	Q3					
	Q4					
2022	Q1					
	Q2					
	Q3					
	Q4					

Once you've accessed, capture the date of the release and enter it in the *Report Date* column. This is of minor importance, but it will serve to alert you when quarterly reports for the *next* year might be due for release.

Select Columns D and F, then select *Number, Decimal Place 0* and *Use 1000 Separator*. Select Columns E and G, then select *Number, Percentage, Decimal Place 0/*

In Column D, Row 8, enter the Forecast numbers from the Press Release.

In Column F Row 8, enter the Revenue numbers from the Press Release. If not already entered, capture and enter the Revenues for the year ago quarter in Column F Row 4.\

In Column E, Row 8, enter the following formula:

=(D8-E4)/E4

In Column G, Row 4, enter the following formula:

=(G8-G4)/G4

Comparing the entries in E8 and G8 will reveal how accurate management is in forecasting future performance. Management will typically understate Forecast Revenue, but investors would prefer a credible understatement. If Actual Revenues come in *below* Forecast

Revenue, that would be a red flag and you should then read the *Quarterly Earnings Transcript* in *Seeking Alpha* to ascertain the reason for the shortfall.

*Note: To repeat formulas in any Column, position your cursor in the lower left corner of a cell that contains the original formula. When the cursor becomes a simple plus (+), depress and hold down the **left click** button on your mouse and drag your cursor through all of the Rows in which you want that formula to be active.*

Chapter 9 - Alpha- Beta Investment Strategies

There are moments in history when the science of investing takes a major step forward. Today, another investing revolution is afoot: Alpha/Beta separation.

"Betting or Beta?", Journal Of Indexing, March/April 2009

A Brief Primer on Risk/Reward

Perhaps one of the most enduring rules in the world of investing is this: If an investor's objective is to generate higher investment returns, then he or she must assume a higher level of risk. Conversely, if one's investment objective is to lower risk, then one must assume a lower investment return. Pursuing higher returns with lower risks has often represented an impossible dream in the world of investing.

The reason for this enduring rule can be easily illustrated. Some of the safest investments in the world are bonds issued by the U.S. government. Because of that perceived safety, there is usually a large demand for those bonds. When buying bonds, investors are essentially buying yield or income. Therefore, the heightened demand for those bonds keeps the yield comparatively low. Due to the perception of incomparable safety, the U.S. government does not have to issue bonds with a high interest rate to attract investors.

In contrast, a corporate bond – which inherently is riskier than a U.S. government bond – must have a higher yield to create or increase the demand from investors. If the risk of a corporate bond is perceived to be high, then the yield will have to be commensurately high. Investors will insist on higher rates of return to compensate for the implied risk they are taking.

How is the concept of risk and reward revealed in the world of stocks? Here again, stocks that are perceived to have a low level of risk – for example, so-called Blue-Chip stocks like Exxon Mobil, General Motors, AT&T, and Bank of America - usually have a lower potential for market appreciation than stocks that are perceived to have a higher level of risk.

To illustrate, stocks that comprise the Standard & Poor's 500 Index (S&P 500) are widely followed, widely analyzed, and widely owned by institutional and individual investors. These companies seldom issue financial reports that have not been anticipated by investors. They tend to epitomize the efficient market theory – the market prices reflect all that is known about the present and the future financial performance of those companies. So, from the perspective that there is a low likelihood of negative financial surprises, they are deemed to have a low level of risk. The reward for investing in these stocks is typically limited to the movement of the overall market.

In contrast, stocks that are not widely followed or widely analyzed and widely owned by institutional and individual investors do represent a significant element of risk since there is considerably less known about the present and the future performance of these companies as compared to companies in the S&P 500. This lack of knowledge does not necessarily mean that their future is inherently risky – they're simply not as widely known, therefore the possible risk of negative financial surprises has not yet been reduced.

That lack of knowledge quite often equates to lower current market values vis-à-vis the potential for higher-than-average future market values. Said differently, investors who are among the first to diligently research and successfully identify the winners among these lesser-known companies will usually reap above-average rewards.

Enter Alpha/Beta Separation

Using the concept of Alpha/Beta separation, many of the nation's largest institutional investment managers believe that they have developed an investment strategy that enables them to increase their investment returns while decreasing their level of risk.

What is Alpha/Beta separation? It is the coupling of two unique but contrasting investment strategies within a single portfolio. It is achieved by allocating one part of a portfolio to a Beta strategy and the other part of the portfolio to an Alpha strategy. Therefore, one portfolio essentially achieves Alpha/Beta separation. When this concept is effectively executed, the result is often a reduction of risk (Beta) and an increase in returns (Alpha).

A Beta investment strategy is achieved by generating investment returns that closely track the performance of the market. For example, if the overall market advances 15%, a portfolio dedicated to a Beta investment strategy will usually advance roughly 15%. It also works in reverse, i.e., when the overall market declines, a portfolio dedicated to a Beta investment strategy will usually decline by a percentage roughly equal to that of the market.

An Alpha investment strategy is not related to the overall movement of the market but, rather, reflects the skill involved in picking stocks, whether through market timing or insightful analysis. Alpha investment strategies offer investors the opportunity to achieve better than market average investment performance.

The percentage of a portfolio that is dedicated to each of the two separate strategies is usually determined by assessing the appetite for reward and aversion to risk for each investor. This process is an art, not a science, and basically attempts to determine how much risk an investor is willing to assume to increase investment returns.

If the aversion to risk is high, then the percentage of a portfolio dedicated to Beta strategies will be higher than the percentage dedicated to Alpha strategies. If the investment objective is for higher investment returns, then the percentage of a portfolio dedicated to Alpha strategies will be higher than the percentage dedicated to Beta strategies.

Most of the nation's largest institutional investment managers are uniquely endowed with awesome levels of assets under management and unrivaled research capabilities. These qualities allow institutional investment managers to divide their portfolios between Alpha and Beta investment strategies. Those unique institutional investor characteristics are rarely found in the portfolios of individual investors, therefore individual investors are often precluded from pursuing the same strategies used by institutional investors to achieve Alpha/Beta separation.

The awesome levels of assets under management enable larger institutional investment managers to allocate a percentage of their portfolios to core stocks – stocks like GE, IBM, INTC, MSFT, XOM, etc. Most of these stocks are components of the S&P 500. Therefore, those holdings, virtually by definition, enable the largest institutional investment managers to effectively track the performance of the overall market. This broad diversification involves lower risk than investing in just one or even a handful of different stocks. Essentially it reduces the risk of investing to the performance of the overall market and thereby delivers Beta performance.

The largest institutional investment managers and hedge funds have unrivaled research capabilities, led by teams of experienced and discerning analysts whose full-time job is to discover tomorrow's winning stocks – today. Given the highly competitive industry of institutional investing, there is an obvious imperative to discover stocks that have the potential to perform better than the market averages. When tomorrow's winning stocks are discovered – today, they deliver Alpha performance.

Fortunately, there are investment alternatives available to individual investors and their investment advisors that will enable them to achieve virtually the same Alpha/Beta separation in their individual portfolios that larger institutional investors achieve in their portfolios.

When individual investors and their investment advisors effectively implement Alpha/Beta separation in their individual portfolios, they will also achieve the two heretofore mutually exclusive investment goals of lower risks and higher returns.

Beta Investment Strategy for Individual Investors

Individual investors are not likely to have enough assets to build a portfolio with all of the core stocks owned by the largest institutional investment managers. However, there are effective alternatives that will provide individual investors with the same Beta performance enjoyed by those investment managers.

One potential Beta performance alternative for individual investors is an *Index Fund* that mirrors the performance of the overall market.

Another potential Beta performance alternative for individual investors is an *Exchange Traded Fund* (ETF) that tracks the performance of the overall market. ETFs offer investors the opportunity to focus their investments on specific segments of the market, as well as on the overall market.

Some of America's most respected investment gurus have recommended that individuals should invest in Index funds for the bulk of their portfolios. Consider the following:

"Most investors, both institutional and individual, will find that the best way to own common stocks is through an index fund that charges minimal fees. Those following this path are sure to beat the net results (after fees and expenses) delivered by the great majority of investment professionals."

Warren Buffett's 1997 Investment Letter to Shareholders

Other advocates of index funds include investment luminaries such as Peter Lynch, Charles Schwab, James Cramer and – of course, the man who created the index fund concept in the mid-'80s – John Bogle. Interestingly, Charles Schwab has said that roughly 75% of his investment assets are in index funds.

If you are unsure about which index fund or market tracking ETF might be best for you, consider the advice offered by a successful institutional investor, **David Swensen** – who has been Yale University's Chief Investment Officer since 1985 – in an interview for Barron's:

Q: What's the best index for getting exposure to U.S. stocks, the S&P 500?

A: No, the Wilshire 5000. It is supposed to represent every marketable security out there, whereas the S&P 500 is a large-cap index. For individual investors, broader is better.

Other ETFs that focus on industry sectors, geographic regions, countries and investing styles offer greater diversification – and therefore less risk – than buying individual stocks. However, they do not offer the broader diversification – and lower risk – of market-tracking ETFs or an Index Fund. Therefore, I recommend that individual investors use market-tracking ETFs or a market tracking Index Fund to achieve Beta performance when structuring their portfolios.

Although Index Funds – as well as market-tracking Exchange Traded Funds (ETFs) – offer individual investors the opportunity to match the performance of the market at a very low cost, the best they offer individual or institutional investors is average performance. Index funds and market-tracking ETFs offer zero potential for owning a specific stock that might generate significant Alpha performance and thereby increase any investor's portfolio performance.

Although other ETFs – those that focus on industry sectors, geographic regions, countries and investing styles – offer the potential to achieve higher returns than market-tracking ETFs, they are also constrained by generating an *average* performance of the stocks that comprise each ETF. Said differently, a portfolio that invests in the *top performing stocks* that might be included in one of these *other* ETFs would obviously generate higher investment returns than investing in the ETF which included those top performing stocks – along with a host of other stocks.

Can Individual Investors Achieve Alpha/Beta Separation With Mutual Funds?

According to John Bogle, the inevitable consequence of turning over investment assets to a mutual fund is – at best – average performance. In fact, there are metrics involved with this sort of passive investment that almost guarantee below average performance. Here's what Bogle had to say about the unavoidably negative performance of mutual funds:

During the period 1984–2004, the average fund lagged the market by 3.1 percentage points per year. While the U.S. stock market, as measured by the Standard & Poor's 500 Stock Index, provided an annual rate of return of 13.0 percent, the return on the average equity mutual fund was 9.9 percent. Don't be surprised. That's just what we should have expected.

That gap may seem small. But when the returns are compounded, the gap reaches stunning proportions. An initial investment of $10,000, simply invested in the stock market in 1984, would have produced a profit of $105,200, twenty years later. The profit on the same investment, made in the average mutual fund, would have come to just $56,100.

So, here's the situation: you, the investor, put up 100 percent of the capital and assumed 100 percent of the risk, but collected only 53 percent of the profit. The mutual fund management and distribution system put up zero percent of the capital and assumed zero percent of the risk but collected 47 percent of the return. Almost half of the profit was siphoned away by those who had everything to gain, and nothing to lose.

Remarks by John C. Bogle, *Founder and Former Chairman, The Vanguard Group*
The World Money Show, February 2, 2005

Have mutual funds performed any better in recent years? Consider the following:

"Last year was a great one for the U.S. stock market. It was another disappointment for stock-picking fund managers.

Fueled by rip-roaring corporate profits and easy monetary policy, the benchmark S&P 500 notched a total return, including price gains and dividends, of 28.7% last year.

*That was a stronger showing than that of **85%** of U.S. large-cap stock-picking mutual funds, according to data from S&P Dow Jones Indices.*

*The failure of stock pickers to beat the benchmark is nothing new: 2021 was the **12th consecutive year** in which most actively managed funds of large-cap stocks watched the S&P 500 pass them by."*

Stock Pickers Watched S&P 500 Pass Them by Again in 2021, **The Wall Street Journal**, *March 17, 2022*

Can one assume that the performance of investment managers would be different and better than the performance of mutual fund managers? **Jack Meyer**, the remarkably successful wizard who tripled the **Harvard Endowment Fund** from $8 billion to $27 billion offers the following:

"Most people think they can find investment managers who can outperform, but most people are wrong. I will say that 85 percent to 90 percent of investment managers fail to match their benchmarks. Because managers have fees and incur transaction costs, you know that in the aggregate they are deleting value."

Before we all decide to abandon our active management strategies, it's important to recognize that if all investors embraced a passive investment strategy, markets would lose their viability. The critical market process of allocating capital to the most constructive business opportunities would be greatly diminished. Fortunately, most of the nation's leading institutional investment management firms and hedge funds are firmly committed to active investment management.

They are irrevocably committed to discovering stocks with Alpha potential. They are committed to the concept of discovering tomorrow's winning stocks . . . today.

And that's what I've tried to accomplish with this book – helping individual and smaller institutional investors in their quest to discover stocks with Alpha potential . . . helping them to discover tomorrow's winning stocks . . . *today*.

Chapter 10 – Digital Transformation Books

Content descriptions for each book are taken from *Amazon.com*. For eBook readers, select italicized/underlined content for direct access to books on *Amazon.com*

The Second Machine Age - Erik Brynjolfsson, Andrew McAfee

In recent years, Google's autonomous cars have logged thousands of miles on American highways and IBM's Watson trounced the best human *Jeopardy!* players. Digital technologies — with hardware, software, and networks at their core — will in the near future diagnose diseases more accurately than doctors can, apply enormous data sets to transform retailing, and accomplish many tasks once considered uniquely human. In *The Second Machine Age* MIT's Erik Brynjolfsson and Andrew McAfee — two thinkers at the forefront of their field — reveal the forces driving the reinvention of our lives and our economy. As the full impact of digital technologies is felt, we will realize immense bounty in the form of dazzling personal technology, advanced infrastructure, and near-boundless access to the cultural items that enrich our lives. Amid this bounty will also be wrenching change. Professions of all kinds — from lawyers to truck drivers — will be forever upended. Companies will be forced to transform or die. Recent economic indicators reflect this shift: Fewer people are working, and wages are falling even as productivity and profits soar.

The Inevitable: Understanding the 12 Technological Forces That Will Shape Our Future – Kevin Kelly

Much of what will happen in the next 30 years is inevitable, driven by technological trends that are already in motion. In this fascinating, provocative new book, Kevin Kelly provides an optimistic road map for the future, showing how the coming changes in our lives - from virtual reality in the home to an on-demand economy to artificial intelligence embedded in everything we manufacture - can be understood as the result of a few long-term, accelerating forces. Kelly both describes these deep trends - interacting, cognifying, flowing, screening, accessing, sharing, filtering, remixing, tracking, and questioning - and demonstrates how they overlap and are codependent on one another.

Abundance: The Future Is Better Than You You Think – Peter H. Diamandis

In Abundance, space entrepreneur turned innovation pioneer Peter H. Diamandis and award-winning science writer Steven Kotler document how progress in artificial intelligence, robotics, digital manufacturing synthetic biology, and other exponentially growing technologies will enable us to make greater gains in the next two decades than we have in the previous 200 years. We will soon have the ability to meet and exceed the basic needs of every person on the planet. Abundance for all is within our grasp.

The Four – Scott Galloway

For all that's been written about the *Amazon, Apple, Facebook and Google* over the last two decades, no one has captured their power and staggering success as insightfully as Scott Galloway. Instead of buying the myths these companies broadcast, Galloway asks fundamental questions. How did the Four infiltrate our lives so completely that they're almost impossible to avoid (or boycott)? Why does the stock market forgive them for sins that would destroy other firms? And as they race to become the world's first trillion-dollar company, can anyone challenge them? In the same irreverent style that has made him one of the world's most celebrated business professors, Galloway deconstructs the strategies of the Four that lurk beneath their shiny veneers. He shows how they manipulate the fundamental emotional needs that have driven us since our ancestors lived in caves, at a speed and scope others can't match. And he reveals how you can apply the lessons of their ascent to your own business or career.

Machine, Platform, Crowd: Harnessing Our Digital Future –
Andrew McAfee, Erik Brynjolfsson

In The Second Machine Age, Andrew McAfee and Erik
Brynjolfsson predicted some of the far-reaching effects of digital
technologies on our lives and businesses. Now they've written a
guide to help listeners make the most of our collective
future. Machine | Platform | Crowd outlines the opportunities and
challenges inherent in the science fiction technologies that have
come to life in recent years, like self-driving cars and 3D printers,
online platforms for renting outfits and scheduling workouts, or
crowd-sourced medical research and financial instruments.

*Winners Take All – The 9 Fundamental Rules of High Tech
Strategy* – Tony Seba

'Winners Take All' shows the strategies and tactics, the business
and marketing rules that Google, Apple, Symantec, Netflix,
Salesforce, Craigslist, LinkedIn, Skype, StarMine, Clickability, F5,
IBM, and others have used to build their products, services, and
companies into winners and how they have achieved success in the
high-speed, high-greed, hyper-competitive world that creates new
industries, transforms old ones, and generates unimaginable new
wealth in no time flat: Silicon Valley. Written by a successful
Silicon Valley entrepreneur, lecturer at Stanford University, business
architect, mentor capitalist, consultant and advisor and mentor to
CEOs and entrepreneurs, this book contains the strategies, analytical
templates, step-by-step implementation frameworks, and tools that
these winners have successfully used to build their billion-dollar
companies. The virtual 'Winners Take All' portfolio (see
http://www.tonyseba.com) had returns that widely exceeded the
competition and the market.

AI Superpowers: China, Silicon Valley, and the New World Order
– Kai-Fu-Lee

In AI Superpowers, Kai-fu Lee argues powerfully that because of
these unprecedented developments in AI, dramatic changes will be
happening much sooner than many of us expected. Indeed, as the

US-Sino AI competition begins to heat up, Lee urges the US and China to both accept and to embrace the great responsibilities that come with significant technological power. Most experts already say that AI will have a devastating impact on blue-collar jobs. But Lee predicts that Chinese and American AI will have a strong impact on white-collar jobs as well. Is universal basic income the solution? In Lee's opinion, probably not. But he provides a clear description of which jobs will be affected and how soon, which jobs can be enhanced with AI, and most importantly, how we can provide solutions to some of the most profound changes in human history that are coming soon.

Digital Transformation: Survive and Thrive in an Era of Mass Extinction – Thomas M. Siebel

The confluence of four technologies - elastic cloud computing, big data, artificial intelligence, and the internet of things - writes Siebel, is fundamentally changing how business and government will operate in the 21st century. Siebel masterfully guides listeners through a fascinating discussion of the game-changing technologies driving digital transformation and provides a roadmap to seize them as a strategic opportunity. He shows how leading enterprises such as Enel, 3M, Royal Dutch Shell, the US Department of Defense, and others are applying AI and IoT with stunning results. Digital Transformation is the guidebook every business and government leader needs to survive and thrive in the new digital age.

\

Made in the USA
Middletown, DE
17 November 2022

15151509R00060